THE SALES SHOT

THE SALES SHOT

100 FAST PACED, HARD HITTING SALES TIPS

Sean P. Leahy

Library of Congress Control Number: 2012913170
ISBN: Hardcover   978-1-4771-4825-9
                 Softcover   978-1-4771-4824-2
                 Ebook   978-1-4771-4826-6

This book was printed in the United States of America.

Copyedited by Jan Denn Arriba.
Reviewed by Ryan Cortes.

Rev. date: 04/29/2013

To order additional copies of this book, contact:
Xlibris Corporation
1-888-795-4274
www.Xlibris.com
Orders@Xlibris.com
117026

TABLE OF CONTENTS

ACKNOWLEDGMENTS

First, thank you to my wife, Donna, and my three children, Kristine, Ryan, and Cameron. Thank you all for putting up with my crazy ideas and crazier stories. Donna and Kristine, thanks for editing and advising as this book developed. Ryan, thanks for all the deep and thought-provoking conversations and for challenging me to improve. And Cam, thanks for designing *The Sales Shot* logo and cover.

Thank you to my mom, Irene Van Riper, for being the most inspirational mother in the history of motherhood. Thank you for working three jobs to support our family but for always having more time to love your kids. You are an amazing woman!

To my dad, who is no longer with us, thank you for exposing me to the world of sales, for allowing me to ride with you while you sold janitorial supplies in New York, and for dropping me off to sell jewelry on the streets outside of Rockefeller Center.

Thanks to my brother and sister, Kevin and Robyn, for always being smarter than me but for never making me feel stupid. But mostly, thanks for being the most supportive, caring, loving brother and sister a kid can have.

Thank you to the endless people who inspired stories both inside and outside of this book. Many of you have been named, some of you have not. Nevertheless, all of you have taught me valuable lessons that I will cherish forever.

Thank you to Don Whiteman, Chuck Steiner, Marty Burbridge, Carl Otterness, and Vince Nall, all of whom I have worked for and learned the most from. Without exception, you all taught me a ton about business but even more about life.

Thank you to Deb DiSandro for all of the invaluable advice on how to write and publish a book.

And finally to Bob Horn, Joe Howley, and Brian Leahy...your eternal optimism was absolutely amazing. I really miss you.

INTRODUCTION

This shot is for you! It's quick, it's concise, and it's impactful.

If you are in business today, you don't have a lot of extra time on your hands. That is why this book is designed to give you fast paced, hard hitting, sales tips that you can consume easily and quickly.

You can read the book from cover to cover, or you can use the table of contents to pick and choose what to read.

Each "Sales Shot" tells you how the average salesperson handles a situation and what the "sales superstar" does differently.

No matter how you use the book, I hope it helps you to be a sales superstar!

Enjoy!

SECTION I
SALESPEOPLE ARE LIKE FIGHTER PILOTS

1. Salespeople are like fighter pilots

Salespeople are to their company what fighter pilots are to the air force. They are both the backbones of their organizations, and they both determine the success or failure of everyone who supports them.

No other position is as critical to a company as the sales position. But with the importance comes responsibility.

In order to study the enemy, work on new strategy, and learn about new weapons and tactics, a veteran fighter pilot trains for hours each week. As the "fighter pilot" of your company, you must do the same.

What the *average salesperson* does:

The average salesperson believes his experience will be enough to succeed. He feels that education helped him get his job, but now that he has it, training is no longer necessary. Unfortunately, if he is not improving, he is regressing.

What the *sales superstar* does:

The sales superstar embraces the need for continuous improvement. He attends training sessions, works on strategy, reads sales books, and listens to sales training while in his car. He constantly seeks ways to sharpen his skills and maintain a competitive advantage.

1

What can you do?

Focus on three areas: product knowledge, market knowledge, and sales skills. Each week or month, dedicate yourself to work on one area. Challenge yourself to think like a fighter pilot and constantly sharpen your skills. Buy a sales book, a podcast, or attend a training class; you will have a more successful year if you do!

SECTION II
ONLY SELLING IS SELLING

2. No One Wants to be a Salesperson

During my senior year of college I joined about 100 of my fellow students at a career seminar lead by a local business leader. I don't remember much that he said but I do remember this. He asked the audience a series of questions about what they wanted to do once they graduated.

"How many of you want to be managers?" A bunch of kids raised their hands.

"How many Accountants?" A few raised their hands.

And so on and so on until he asked "How many of you want to be a Salesperson?" Me and some other kid raised our hands. Everyone looked at us and laughed.

The presenter went on to say that only 2% of college students wanted to be salespeople and based on his little survey, the statistic appeared to be true. His next statement shocked everyone though.

"Over 50% of CEO's in America come up through sales." That is a fact that continues to be true today.

What the *average salesperson* does:

The average salesperson falls into sales as a last resort.

What the *sales superstar* does:

The Sales Superstar is PROUD to be a Salesperson.

What can you do?

It is no accident that most CEO's come up through the Sales Department. Unlike any other position in a company, salespeople tend to be more self-motivated, more knowledgeable of all aspects of their own company, their competition, and the market. Salespeople tend to be better communicators, more resilient, and more aggressive. They also tend to have more responsibility, greater career satisfaction, and make more money than their peers. As it turns out, Sales is a great profession! Be proud of it!!!

3. Only Selling Is Selling

Chris Clarke Epstein, author of eleven books, once told a group of aspiring authors, "Only writing is writing." She said that most writers fail because they waste time on activities other than the one that helps them succeed—writing!

Salespeople are similar to writers. A study by Proudfoot Consulting found that the average salesperson spends only 10 percent of their time selling face-to-face with customers. The largest amount of their time (31 percent) was dedicated to administration. Travel time (18 percent) and "downtime" (17 percent) ranked well above actual sales time.

Other studies have shown that a salesperson's success grows exponentially with the amount of time they are face-to-face with a customer.

What the *average salesperson* does:

The average salesperson gets distracted and spends far too much time on nonselling activity.

What the *sales superstar* does:

The superstar understands where the money comes from. She eliminates downtime, reduces administrative time, and increases *selling* time.

What can you do?

Live by the motto "Only *selling* is *selling*"! Keep a log for one week and record the time you are in front of a customer. Then divide that by the number of hours you worked that week to determine your percentage of *selling* time. If you are below 30 percent, you must work to eliminate downtime, travel time, administrative time, and wasted time. Then you must replace it with face-to-face time.

4. Perennial Planners

On Monday morning, Jim the salesman sat down to plan his week. His sales manager was happy to see Jim planning.

On Tuesday, his manager asked Jim what he was doing. Jim said he was reworking his plan.

On Wednesday, the manager was not pleased to learn that Jim needed to start his plan over.

Thursday came and Jim was "adding the final touches."

On Friday, Jim was fired!

What the *average salesperson* does:

Jim was not average. Jim stunk! Jim "never left the locker room." The average salesperson at least takes some risk and plays the game. The "bad" salesperson finds every excuse imaginable to sit around his desk and not see customers.

What the *sales superstar* does:

The superstar plans but then goes out, knowing full well that his plan is not perfect. He knows that he can't win unless he is asking for an order . . . and he can't ask for an order while sitting around planning how to do it!

What can you do?

Every week, give yourself a "start time" just like an athlete has a start time for a game. Your start time is when your planning time must end and your selling time must start. Whether your plan for the week is finished or not, stop your planning and start your selling!

5. Focus

If you were a rhinoceros hunter, what would you do with your gun when you come across a two-ton rhino? Would you look for an elephant to shoot? Would you shoot a deer?

Would you call your boss, check your e-mail, or do some paperwork? No, you would *focus* on the rhino and shoot it!

That is exactly how you must approach selling. Eliminate all activity that does not directly result in your success and then focus all your energy on what does.

What the *average salesperson* does:

The average salesperson tends to chase all opportunities. He reacts to the pressure of needing sales and goes after every opportunity that presents itself. He is easily distracted and spends more time answering e-mails, doing paperwork, and being unproductive than he does pursuing business that will deliver sales.

What the *sales superstar* does:

The superstar first identifies his rhinoceros. He knows where the business is that will deliver what he needs, and then he pursues it with a vengeance. He eliminates distractions and focuses all his energy on his target.

What can you do?

You can do two things. First, narrow down what you have to do to succeed to three, and only three, things. Make sure that all three of those things will deliver sales, period.

Second, eliminate your distractions and pursue these three things with a vengeance. If you do just a few things extremely well, you will be much more successful than if you do twelve things halfheartedly.

6. I Have All Their Business

The famous last words of the salesperson are "I have all their business."

If your life depended on getting a sale, where would you turn? Would you go to an existing customer or would you try to get a brand new one? Hopefully you said you would go to an existing customer, because that is where you have the greatest odds for success.

The odds of getting an order from a customer you have never done business with before are 14:1. The odds improve to 4:1 for a customer you have done business with in the past, and when you're working with an existing customer, the odds are 2:1.

Unfortunately, many salespeople believe they already have all their current customers business. At the same time, close to 80 percent of customers say that's not true!

What the *average salesperson* does:

The average salesperson assumes he has maximized his existing customers' potential and leaves the opportunity of new business to his competitors.

What the *sales superstar* does:

The sales superstar realizes that his greatest chance for success is with those whom he already has an established relationship. He relentlessly pursues opportunities to expand his business with existing customers and increases his odds of success from 14:1 to 2:1.

What can you do?

You can "sniff the plant"! In the industrial world, this means getting past the buyer and into their manufacturing "plant" so you can "sniff" around for opportunities to sell more products. No matter what business you are in, the key is to find out what other products or services you can sell to your existing customer. Oftentimes they are anxious to consolidate their business to you. It's a lot easier than cracking a completely new account!

7. The Tournament

Success comes from focusing more on less and less on more. Or, as Steve Jobs puts it, "Get rid of the crappy stuff and focus on the good stuff."

A lot has been written about the success of Apple and Southwest Airlines, but one commonality between the two stands out as to why they achieved greatness. Focus!

In 1998, when Apple was struggling, Steve Jobs reduced the number of products Apple sold from three hundred fifty to ten. The company skyrocketed.

Southwest had one type of airplane, the Boeing 737. As a result, their supply chain is simpler, their training is easier, their inventory is lower, and their service levels and profit margins are higher. The motto at Southwest is "Do what you're good at."

What the *average salesperson* does:

The average salesperson gets distracted. He chases after every opportunity that comes his way rather than focusing on the good stuff.

What the *sales superstar* does:

The superstar focuses on what he is good at and gets rid of the crappy stuff.

What can you do?

Use my tournament method to force yourself to identify what you need to focus on. Here is how it works:

1. Brainstorm. Create a list of everything you can think of that you can do in order to attain you goal for the year.

2. Create a "bracket" similar to an NCAA basketball tournament. See a sample on the next page.

3. Enter each idea from your brainstorm list into the tournament.

4. Each "bracket" becomes a contest where only one entry advances to the next round. Answer the question "If I can only do one of these, which would it be?" The answer advances.

5. Continue this process to determine your top three priorities.

6. Focus on these three activities and dramatically increase your chances for success.

Your chances for success are much greater if you do one thing extremely well versus doing ten things fairly well.

This process works for prioritizing everything from strategy to where to go on your family vacation.

Tournament

Your Focus

TARGET "A's"

"A's"

QUESTIONS

UPPER MGT.

TARGET "A's"

CUSTOMIZE

QUESTIONS

1. UPPER MGT.

8. PRIORITIZE

3. TARGET "A's"

6. CUSTOMIZE

4. FIRE BAD COSTS

5. ATTACK

2. FACE TIME

7. QUESTIONS

1. CALL ON UPPER MGT.

2. INCREASE FACE TIME

3. TARGET "A" ACCOUNTS

4. FIRE BAD CUSTOMERS

5. ATTACK COMPETITORS

6. CUSTOMIZE PRESENTATIONS

7. ASK BETTER QUESTIONS

8. PRIORITIZE

To download a full-size original copy of The Tournament,
go to www.seanleahy.com/handouts.

8. ChecklistEvery Sales Call

Because pilots do the very same safety checks every time they fly, they use a checklist to make sure they don't miss a step. After performing the same steps thousands of times you would think they would remember what to do without a checklist, wouldn't you?

Well, no! Because they do it over and over again, that is exactly the reason they need a checklist.

Checklists are also excellent tools for the veteran salesperson. You will find a checklist for every sales call on the next page. You can also order a complete pocket-size checklist, including checklists for negotiations, creating a PowerPoint presentation, calling on upper management, sales questions, and every sales call by going to www.seanleahy.com/sales-checklist.

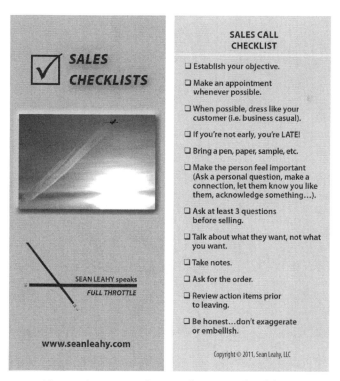

To receive a complete pocket-size checklist, go to www.seanleahy.com/sales-checklist.

SECTION III
ITS ABOUT THEM

9. About Us

If your first PowerPoint slide is about your company, change it!

Think about it—a PowerPoint presentation is no different than a typical sales call, except it is to more than one person. And since you are using PowerPoint, it probably means that you are leading a very important sales presentation.

So if you wouldn't start a sales call by telling your customer a bunch of boring facts about you and your company, you shouldn't start your PowerPoint presentation that way either.

What the *average salesperson* does:

The average salesperson uses the standard company presentation and reluctantly presents the same slides every time. Most times, the first or second slide is titled something like "About Us."

What the *sales superstar* does:

The superstar customizes and personalizes each presentation. Rather than losing the audience by providing boring information about his own company, the superstar starts with information about his customer. This technique gains the attention of his audience and shows them that their needs are the focus. He immediately differentiates himself from his competition.

What can you do?

Try doing what Dave Branning of Infoprint Solutions does. Steve starts his presentations by saying, "OK, enough about me, let's talk about *you*." Not only does he get a laugh, he lets his customer know that they are his focus.

At the very least, start by getting rid of the "About Us" slide. Replace it with any of the following: "What I Understand About You," "Your Priorities," or anything about your customer. They will be glad you did!

10. Red Roses

Every Valentine's Day, men everywhere buy roses for the women in their lives. And an overwhelming number of those men buy *red* roses. Unfortunately, a significant majority of women prefer a color other than red when they receive roses from a man. Those same women rarely, if ever, tell those men of their preference.

Why is this important? Because if a man is buying roses for someone, it probably means he knows her pretty well. And if he knows her well, one can assume he knows what color rose she likes. But he probably doesn't. The best way for him to find out is to ask her.

What is the moral of this story? Salespeople often think they know their customers pretty well too. Oftentimes they don't know them quite as well as they think.

What the *average salesperson* does:

The average salesperson assumes he knows everything about his customers. He neglects to ask probing questions, and he doesn't know when his customer changes his opinion.

What the *sales superstar* does:

The superstar keeps asking questions. He knows that people have changing needs and wants, and he knows it is better to ask than to assume. And most importantly, when he truly knows what his customer wants, he delivers exactly the right solution.

What can you do?

If you are a man who may buy roses for Valentine's Day, go ahead and ask the question. Ask her if she were to receive roses this year, what color she would prefer. Then deliver exactly the roses she wants. If it works, then do the same with your customers.

If you are a woman who would like to receive roses this year, go ahead and tell him what color you would prefer. But just because he may not have asked the question does not mean you should do the same with your customers.

11. Dont Buy That Stereo

I walked into my fourth stereo store in search of the perfect stereo. While looking at a receiver, I heard the salesman say, "Don't buy that stereo." He got my attention!

He followed with "Can I ask you a few questions before I recommend the best equipment for you?"

I of course said, "Yes."

He then asked me where I was going to put the stereo, how big the room was, what kind of music I liked, how loud I liked to play it . . . and so on and so on.

By the time he was done, he knew more about what I wanted than I knew what I wanted. When he suggested what I should buy . . . I bought it!

What the *average salesperson* does:

The average salesperson tells his benefit story so often that it becomes routine. He forgets, however, that the purchase is very unique for the customer. And the customer wants to feel that his unique wants are understood before the salesperson makes a recommendation.

What the *sales superstar* does:

The superstar makes his customer feel special by taking the time to ask all the questions and to understand exactly what the customer needs. Then, and only then, does he suggest a solution.

What can you do?

If a stereo salesperson can do this successfully, can't you? Don't assume that you know all the answers because you have dealt with a customer for a long time—that is what your competition is doing. Keep asking the questions. Not only will it reinforce that you care about what they want, you will also keep learning what they need.

12. Ask Questions and Listen

Many salespeople act as if they are married to their customers. They use terms like "partner" or "sleeping with my customer" to describe their relationship.

The problem is, according to statistics, most marriages either end in divorce . . . or should. Unfortunately, the same is happening with customers who are making tough choices and divorcing suppliers they have been "married" to for years.

What the *average salesperson* does:

The average salesperson treats their customer like the person in a failing marriage treats their spouse. They get comfortable in the relationship, focus on their own needs and problems first, and forget to pay attention to what's important to their "partner."

The average salesperson starts a meeting by telling the customer their problems and acts as if the customer is there to help them instead of the other way around.

What the *sales superstar* does:

The superstar listens! The superstar asks questions and finds out what is impacting the customer and their life. They let their customer know that the customer's needs and situation are more important than their own needs are. And then they do something about it.

What can you do?

Trust me, your customers' problems are more important to them than yours are. And they are much more likely to buy what you are selling if they believe you are concerned with what they need.

So take a deep breath, and try to picture your spouse the next time you see your customers, and get inside their head to understand their needs first.

Your intelligence is determined more by the quality of the questions you ask than the quality of the statements you make.

13. The Top Three Sales Questions

You just had another conversation with your boss about your need to increase sales . . . now. He needs to close the year out strong.

So what do you do?

What the *average salesperson* does:

The average salesperson forgets everything he knows and starts selling, selling, selling. And the way he does that is by talking, talking, talking.

What the *sales superstar* does:

The superstar confidently asks *questions*, for it is asking the right questions that uncover opportunity. Here are *three powerful questions* that will help sell more:

1. *"What is keeping you up at night?"* The reason this question is important is because (a) it is about their business, not yours; (b) you learn things about their overall business, which gives you insight on how to solve their most critical issues; and (c) you often get personal answers about their lives, which helps you enhance your relationship. This question encourages answers unlike any other.

2. *"If you were me, what would you do?"* This question cuts straight to the point! The answer will tell you exactly what the customers want and how to get their business.

3. *"Why do you do business with us?* It is easy to assume you know the answer to this question, but you may be surprised at the answer. It is important to know the real reasons why a customer buys from you. It will not only help you focus your efforts and negotiate better, it may also help you with other potential customers as well.

What can you do?

Your opportunities come through your ears, not your mouth. So resist the temptation to speak first. These questions will get your customer talking and will provide you with answers you need to get more business. Ask, ask, ask!

14. The Ballet

After years of being a distant second, Jim asked his competitor how he got so tight with his customer. "I take him to the ballet," the competitor said.

"The ballet?" Jim replied with an obvious amount of sarcasm.

"Yes, the ballet!" the competitor answered. "His wife and daughters are ballerinas!"

What the *average salesperson* does:

The average salesperson entertains his customers by doing what he wants to do instead of finding out what would make his customer happy.

What the *sales superstar* does:

The superstar finds out what the customer likes and then separates himself from the competition by entertaining the way the customer wants. So while the other salesmen are all on the golf course, the superstar is writing orders at the ballet.

What can you do?

Chances are, you won't be taking your customer to the ballet, but hopefully you get the point. Everyone is going golfing, or to lunch, or to a sporting event, but if you want to stand out from the crowd, find out what your customer really likes to do but rarely gets a chance to. You might be surprised at the answer.

ChecklistTop Ten Sales Questions

SALES QUESTION CHECKLIST

☐ Ask a personal question. ("How did Jenny's "soccer game" go?" is better than "How are your kids?")

☐ What is keeping you up at night?

☐ If you were me, what would you do?

☐ If there is one thing you really want us to know, what is it?

☐ What do you want to discuss most?

☐ What do you like most about us?

☐ What is the one thing you must have?

☐ What/who prevents you from…?

☐ Who in your company will be affected when you …?

☐ Why?

☐ Is there anything I should have asked you that I haven't yet?

☐ May I have the order?

To receive a complete pocket-size checklist, go to www.seanleahy.com/sales-checklist.

SECTION IV
PRESENTATIONS

15. Begin with the End in Mind

When the Boston Celtics leave their locker room, they see a sign that reads, "Begin with the end in mind."

This Steven Covey message helped the Boston Celtics win seventeen NBA championships, and it can help you win with your customers too.

You can get your customers' attention by starting your sales presentation with the eventual benefit. That way, your customer stays focused in order to hear how you are going to deliver rather than dozing off five minutes in.

What the *average salesperson* does:

The average salesperson leaves the benefit for the end of the presentation, hoping for a strong close. The problem is he might lose the customers' attention along the way.

What the *sales superstar* does:

The superstar starts with a *bang*:

The proposal you are about to see will save you twenty-five thousand dollars this year!

After proclaiming the eventual benefit, the superstar continues his presentation by showing how he will do it. The customer stays focused because he wants to see if the salesperson can prove it.

What can you do?

Whether you're selling one-on-one or making a PowerPoint presentation, begin with the end in mind. Proclaim your ultimate benefit and then prove it. You will keep your customers attention and get a commitment.

16. The Three Parts of a Presentation

The great Dale Carnegie originally defined the sales process as having five distinct steps: attention, interest, desire, conviction, and close. The theory included the fact that the sales process was more effective if the salesperson took these steps in order. If you agree that a presentation is merely a bigger version of a sales call, then you should also agree that it includes these steps.

Unfortunately, only a few people who attend a Dale Carnegie class commit the steps to memory. At the very least, every salesperson should structure a presentation with three parts: opening, body, and close. That is especially true if it is a PowerPoint presentation.

What the *average salesperson* does:

The average salesperson dumps a bunch of facts about his company and product onto PowerPoint slides and then delivers it to a group of people sitting in front of him. When he's finished, he says something like "And that's my presentation."

What the *sales superstar* does:

The superstar organizes his presentation like a sales call with the intention of closing the sale at the end. He starts by grabbing the audiences' attention, builds from there, and finishes by asking for a commitment.

What can you do?

Start with a blank sheet of paper and write down the word *Opening*, followed by *Body*, and then *Close*. Then create an outline by adding what your presentation should include for each one of those steps. Now build your presentation using only slides that support your outline and eliminate any slides that do not.

You will find that your presentation flows more effectively and results in a commitment when you close at the end. Find more specifics on structuring your presentation in the PowerPoint checklist below.

You can also use the presentation planner shown on the next page.

17. Customize, Customize, Customize

If you were having a house built, would you want to have input on the final touches or would you prefer the builder decide everything for you?

When buying a new car, do you want to select the color, the interior, and the gadgets, or would you like the salesperson to pick them?

I suspect you want it to be *your* house and *your* car and would prefer to have it customized your way.

Your customers want the same thing when they buy from you. They will respond much better if you *customize* your presentation to them just like you expect a builder or car salesperson to do.

What the *average salesperson* does:

The average salesperson talks about his product or service *his* way.

What the *sales superstar* does:

The superstar customizes every sales presentation as much as possible and makes it *their* presentation, not his.

SEAN LEAHY speaks
FULL THROTTLE

Presentation Planner

Company:		Contact:	
Date:		Time:	

Objective:

Questions to ask prior to presentation:

1 | *What topics do you want to discuss most?*
Answer:
2
Answer:
3
Answer:

Opening: ☐ Summarize their main interests ☐ State the end benefit ☐ Attention Getter

Only... *(Focus on benefits that are unique to your company)*
Only...
Only...
Only...

Body: ☐ Prove your opening ☐ Make it THEIR presentation ☐ No full sentences ☐ Power of 3

1
   A
   B
   C

2
   A
   B
   C

3
   A
   B
   C

Close: ☐ State your commitment ☐ Solicit their interest ☐ Confirm your solution ☐ Ask for commitment

Before completing presentation preparation, do the following:

☐ For each slide, ask if it can close the deal. If not, cut it! ☐ Ask yourself if they want to hear it more than you want to say it.
☐ Make sure you answered "Why do I want to buy from you?" ☐ Click the spell check button.

To download a full-size original copy of the Presentation Planner, go to www.seanleahy.com/handouts.

What can you do?

First ask all the questions to determine exactly what the customer wants. Then insert every fact you can into your presentation, so it is customized specifically for them. Put on the final touches by using their name, their logo, and their pictures wherever possible. And finally, refer to it as their product, their service, and their presentation throughout the meeting.

18. The Power of Three

When creating or delivering a presentation, use the "power of three."

As children, we were programmed with the ABCs, 123s, and "Three Blind Mice." I could give more examples, but if I went beyond those three, you would lose interest.

As adults, we tell jokes about three guys in a bar; we build paragraphs with a beginning, a middle, and an end; and we rank everything by the top three.

There are reasons why we don't award medals in gold, silver, bronze . . . and nickel.

First, we are programmed to think in threes. Second, we lose interest as soon as a fourth point is given. And third, three unique points can complete a story. The fourth point is usually repeating one of the original three.

What the *average salesperson* does:

The average salesperson feels the need to include every possible piece of information in his presentation.

What the *sales superstar* does:

The superstar consolidates his presentation to the top three points.

What can you do?

Limit your presentations to three major topics. And within those three topics, limit yourself to three bullets or subtopics. Your presentations will appear much more interesting and your audience will stay far more engaged.

19. Can This Close the Deal?

When you finish creating your presentation, you have one last step before hitting the Save button.

Go through every single slide and ask yourself the following question: Can this slide close the deal?

If the answer is no, then you should either omit it or put it in a place where you can only access it if you are asked to.

What the *average salesperson* does:

The average salesperson includes slides that are interesting to him but don't help get the order.

What the *sales superstar* does:

The superstar only includes information that is critical to the success of the meeting.

What can you do?

Understand that the people you are about to present to have seen hundreds of presentations before yours. Most of those presentations included information they had absolutely no interest in.

You will immediately rise to the top if your presentation cuts through all the stuff they don't want to hear about. If it can't close the deal for you, it does not belong in your presentation.

20. Improve Your Image

Old Ad

New Ad

Old Ad

New Ad

What the Average Salesperson does:
(when creating a PowerPoint)

What the Superstar does:
(when creating a PowerPoint)

<u>**Really Important Information**</u>

- This is a really important point so I am going to write it all out in a complete sentence.
- This one must be as important as the last one.
- I would rather you read all of this information so I don't have to say it.
- i just cut this point out of an old presentation because it helped me fill this slide.
- If you have actually read this far you may actually be the only person still awake.
- Maybe I can squeeze yet another boring fact on this page so it looks really full and you start to think that I must be smart to know all of this stuff.

What can you do?

Think about what you just did. You had no interest in reading anything on the left side of this page. But you did seek to figure out the message on the right. Your audience acts the same way.

So improve your image! Be creative. Use images in your presentations to make your point. Then rely on your spoken word, not the printed word.

Advertisers learned this decades ago. It's about time we salespeople do the same!

21. Only . . .

Dedicated—largest—first—committed—superior—world-class—leading. If you use any of these words in your sales presentation, don't! Everybody uses these words!

They are used so much they no longer have any meaning other than to say, "We are just as good as everyone else." Hardly a ringing endorsement.

What the *average salesperson* does:

The average salesperson takes the easy way out and uses average words to describe his company, product, and service.

What the *sales superstar* does:

The superstar uses the word *only*.

What can you do?

Write down these words: *The only...* Then complete the sentence with as many truths about you, your company, product, or service as possible.

> "The *only* company to ship 100 percent complete within one hour."
> "The *only* salesperson to guarantee his . . ."
> "The *only* widget designed by customers."
> "The *only* . . ."

How many ways can you complete that phrase?

It may be a difficult exercise, but it is extremely important to do.

Customers choose a supplier based on their unique abilities, not on what they do as well as everyone else.

If you don't have anything you can say "only" about, you need to start developing some.

ChecklistPowerPoint

POWERPOINT CHECKLIST

☐ Establish the objective.

☐ Ask what they want to hear about, BEFORE preparing presentation.

☐ Opening Options: Summarize their main interests, state the end benefit, create attention getter.

☐ Body - Prove your opening.

☐ Close: State your commitment, solicit their interest, confirm your solution, ask for commitment.

☐ Make it their presentation, not yours (titles, topics, their pictures, etc.).

☐ No paragraphs, no full sentences.

☐ Power of 3: 3 topics, 3 bullets.

☐ Focus on the benefits that are unique to your company. Eliminate benefits anyone can claim, i.e. "Dedicated."

☐ Before completing, ask these questions about every slide.

1. Can this slide close the deal?

2. Do they want to hear this more than I want to say it?

If the answer is "no," cut it.

☐ Click the spellcheck button.

To receive a complete pocket-size checklist, go to www.seanleahy.com/sales-checklist.

SECTION V
YOURE NOT SELLING BREAD, YOURE SELLING PROFIT

22. Youre Not Selling Bread

The year was 1985. Tom Hudak was the number one salesperson in my company, and I was number two. Tom was given an award and asked to give a speech to explain what he did that propelled him to the top.

He told a story that I will never forget, and one which has helped me succeed to this very day. He told how he was pumping gas when a bread truck pulled up to the pump across from him. He asked the driver what he did for a living. Pointing to his truck and the large picture of a loaf of bread, the driver sarcastically said, "I sell bread!"

Tom said, "No you don't! You sell the same thing I do—you sell profit!"

Tom went on to explain that the only reason any business buys anything is so their company eventually makes more profit, period! Otherwise they wouldn't buy your product.

What the *average salesperson* does:

The average salesperson is stuck in the old school. He sells product features and benefits and leaves it at that.

What the *sales superstar* does:

The sales superstar understands the customers' bottom-line motivation is profit! He still sells features and benefits, but he presents how his product or service impacts the customers' bottom line.

What can you do?

Structure your sales presentation to highlight how your customer will make more money with your product versus the competition. Show them how they will save more money and make more money when they buy from you. When you succeed at that, your sales will skyrocket!

23. Profit Margin

If *your* price to *your* customer for *your* product is $18.38, what is *your* profit margin?

"I don't know."

Exactly!

Neither does your customer. And that is the point. Your customer does not know your cost or your profit, so don't be afraid to make some money on the product *you* sell.

What the *average salesperson* does:

The average salesperson (or company) sets pricing based on what the product costs to make or buy. Then he puts a profit margin on top of it.

What the *sales superstar* does:

The superstar sells product based on what the product is *worth*. And when it comes to negotiating, his fist tendency is to sell the value of his product, not concede on price.

What can you do?

Do what Dan Murphy of McNaughton McKay Electric Company does; base your price on the value that you and your product deliver. Don't base it on something the customer doesn't know (cost).

24. Vinces Profit

I never realized how much extra work I had to do when I gave a discount to a customer. That is until the president of the company I worked for at the time, Vince Nall, gave me the table below.

The table shows how much more you need to sell when you cut your price. The highlighted example shows when you have a gross margin of 25 percent and you give an additional 10 percent discount, you will need to sell 66.7 percent extra to make up for the lost margin.

That's a lot!

What the *average salesperson* does:

The average salesperson gives away discounts without thinking about the consequences.

What the *sales superstar* does:

The superstar doesn't mind hard work, but he does mind unnecessary work. So the superstar protects his margin so he can spend his time on additional sales, not making up for lost profit.

What can you do?

Think before you discount. Use the table below whenever you contemplate giving away margin. You will save a lot of selling time if you do.

PM Discount Impact on Profit Margin

Additional Sales Needed to Make up for Discount

Price Cut	PRESENT GROSS PROFIT					
	5.0%	10.0%	15.0%	20.0%	25.0%	30.0%
1%	25.0%	11.1%	7.1%	5.3%	4.2%	3.4%
2%	66.6%	25.0%	15.4%	11.1%	8.7%	7.1%
3%	150.0%	42.8%	25.0%	17.6%	13.6%	11.1%
4%	400.0%	66.6%	36.4%	25.0%	19.0%	15.4%
5%	—.—	100.0%	50.0%	33.3%	25.0%	20.0%
6%	—.—	150.0%	66.7%	42.9%	31.6%	25.0%
7%	—.—	233.3%	87.5%	53.8%	38.9%	30.4%
8%	—.—	400.0%	114.3%	66.7%	47.1%	36.4%
9%	—.—	1000.0%	150.0%	81.8%	56.3%	42.9%
10%	—.—	—.—	200.0%	100.0%	**66.7%**	50.0%
11%	—.—	—.—	275.0%	122.2%	78.6%	57.9%
12%	—.—	—.—	400.0%	150.0%	92.3%	66.7%
13%	—.—	—.—	650.0%	185.7%	108.3%	76.5%
14%	—.—	—.—	1400.0%	233.3%	127.3%	87.5%
15%	—.—	—.—	—.—	300.0%	150.0%	100.0%
16%	—.—	—.—	—.—	400.0%	177.8%	114.3%
17%	—.—	—.—	—.—	566.7%	212.5%	130.8%
18%	—.—	—.—	—.—	900.0%	257.1%	150.0%
19%	—.—	—.—	—.—	1900.0%	316.7%	172.7%
20%	—.—	—.—	—.—	—.—	400.0%	200.0%
21%	—.—	—.—	—.—	—.—	525.0%	233.3%
22%	—.—	—.—	—.—	—.—	733.3%	275.0%
23%	—.—	—.—	—.—	—.—	1115.0%	328.6%
24%	—.—	—.—	—.—	—.—	2400.0%	400.0%
25%	—.—	—.—	—.—	—.—	—.—	500.0%

Additional Sales Needed to Make up for Discount

To download a full-size original copy of Vince's Profit, go to www.seanleahy.com/handouts.

SECTION VI
SELLING INSIDE YOUR OWN HOUSE

25. Selling Inside Your Own House

Charles Plumb was a fighter pilot in Vietnam. In 1967, during his seventy-sixth mission, the enemy shot him down, and he parachuted behind enemy lines. After his capture, Plumb spent six years as a prisoner of war.

Years later, a man approached Plumb and his wife in a restaurant and asked, "Are you Charles Plumb, the navy pilot?"

"Yes, how did you know?" asked Plumb.

"I packed your parachute," the man replied.

Plumb later realized that he never gave thought to this man, or the countless others, whom he depended on for his life.

While your life may not depend on the efforts of your support staff, your livelihood certainly does.

What the *average salesperson* does:

The average salesperson often forgets those who support his selling efforts. He rarely says thank you or acknowledges the impact an inside salesperson, an AR person, or a truck driver has on his success.

What the *sales superstar* does:

The superstar realizes that a buyer only represents one customer, but his support staff impacts every single one of his customers. As a result, the superstar treats his support staff better than anyone else. He seeks ways to show his appreciation to everyone from the person in the warehouse to the person he reports to. In effect, he is "selling inside his own house" even more than he is selling to his customers.

What can you do?

Write down a list of those people who impact your success. Next to their names write down what you can do for them. Then schedule reminders in your calendar to make sure that you don't forget.

26. Quarterback Blitz

An NFL quarterback is judged by how he reacts when a three-hundred-pound lineman blitzes toward him with the force of a freight train. The star quarterback calmly takes a step forward, avoids the tackle, and hits his receiver in stride for a touchdown.

Business leaders are judged by how they handle an onslaught of unexpected challenges as well. The great ones are like the quarterback who doesn't flinch. They show poise and exude confidence. Their employees then trust and follow their lead.

Salespeople are faced with the same challenges.

What the *average salesperson* does:

The average quarterback overreacts, gets nervous, and usually makes a big mistake. Oftentimes he turns around and yells at his teammates as if they were solely to blame. The average salesperson acts the same way when a surprise problem happens. He too overreacts and points the finger of blame at others within his company. He also winds up making big mistakes.

What the *sales superstar* does:

The superstar acts more like the MVP quarterback or the seasoned executive. The superstar remains calm and addresses the problem head on. The confidence he exudes gains the respect and support of the rest of his team and his customer as well.

What can you do?

When you face a bad surprise, think like a quarterback. Don't allow your emotions to take over and definitely don't sell out your teammates.

27. Booger

"Booger."

When the quarterback of a football team disrespects his linemen, some linemen call their own play, they call "booger." Then they all intentionally fail to block anyone, and the quarterback gets sacked so hard he feels like he was hit by a truck!

Most quarterbacks learn the lesson before they lift their weary body off of the turf. They learn that without the support of their teammates, they're "sacked." Those who fail to learn this lesson will never succeed.

What the *average salesperson* does:

Some salespeople fail to realize that everyone who works for his company is like the offensive line that protects their quarterback. He fails to realize they can make or break his success.

What the *sales superstar* does:

The sales superstar treat fellow employees like Dan Marino and Payton Manning treated their offensive lines. They treat them like royalty! Both quarterbacks became famous for buying gifts and taking linemen out to dinner. Marino even bought Rolex watches for his entire offensive line.

What can you do?

You don't have to buy Rolex watches for your inside people, but you can treat your fellow employees like important members of your team. It is no mistake that two of the best quarterbacks in NFL history are both known for how they treated their support staff. If you want to rise to the top, you need to do it too.

SECTION VII
SALES ESSENTIALS

28. Being Prepared

Every flight is off course 99 percent of the time. In order to land at his final destination, a pilot must make constant adjustments from the time the wheels leave the ground to the time the plane lands. That's even tougher for the fighter pilot because his target is constantly moving and usually is fighting back. It is much like a sales call.

The fighter pilot, and the salesperson, increases his chances of success by being overly prepared. He must be prepared for his mission, and he must be prepared for the unexpected as well. Unfortunately, purchasing agents say that less than half of sales people are prepared at all, and less than 10 percent are fully prepared.

What the *average salesperson* does:

The weak salesperson does little to no preparation and then shows up hoping to get an order. He rarely does. Usually he gets "shot down" and wonders why.

What the *sales superstar* does:

The superstar is ready! He has researched the target, he has anticipated the objections, he has all the materials prepared in a format that works best for his customer, and he is prepared for the unexpected. Ultimately, he wins the battle.

What can you do?

Brainstorm and prepare. Before every sales call brainstorm every possibility and everything you need to prepare to guarantee your success. Then act like a fighter pilot and prepare like your life depended on it. Your customer will recognize your effort, and more likely than not, you will win.

29. Do What You Say You Are Going to Do

Have you ever hired someone to do work at your home at a certain time only to have them show up late and act as if it was no big deal? Does it cause you to want to give your business to someone else?

I have asked many customers why they choose one salesperson over another. Very often the answer is "I choose the one who does what he says he is going to do." Some customers say that a salesperson meeting commitments has become the number one differentiator for them in selecting a supplier!

That probably explains why there are hundreds of systems for salespeople to use to manage their promises. From Salesforce.com to the Franklin Planner, every salesperson uses some sort of system to ensure they return a call on time or meet a deadline. So why is it that most customers cite this as a major cause of failure? Because *most* salespeople fail to use the system they have!

What the *average salesperson* does:

The average salesperson does not take the time to write down, or enter in, the commitments he makes into his system.

What the *sales superstar* does:

The superstar makes a commitment his top priority. If he tells someone he is going to do something at a certain time, he sets a *reminder* to ensure he does what he says he is going to do. And that includes the smallest of promises. If you meet those, your customer knows you will meet the big commitments too.

What can you do?

Make sure the system you use has the ability to set reminders. Then *commit* to setting and using the reminder system so when you promise to call in two weeks, you call in two weeks!

30. Go, No-Go?

All salespeople are faced with the decision: Do I go or do I not go? Do I make one more call, or do I go home? Do I make the tough decision, or do I make the easy one?

When you are faced with this decision, do what Theresa Krause of Land O'Lakes does—she goes!

Theresa was a rookie salesperson (livestock production specialist) for Land O'Lakes Feed when she drove up to one of the largest farms in her area. As a rookie, she had never called on a farm this large, and she was nervous about messing up.

She debated, "Should I go . . . or should I go home?

What the *average salesperson* does:

The average salesperson comes up with excuses and finds a reason *not* to go.

What the *sales superstar* does:

The superstar *goes!* The superstar makes the call. That is what Theresa did, and they were thrilled to see her. This farm not only wound up being Theresa's largest customer, they bought more in one month than she had sold the entire year.

What can you do?

You have this debate in your head all the time. You know you do. Imagine the results will be the same as Theresa's and just make the call. You may not win every time, but you will win 100 percent more often than if you choose to go home.

31. If Youre Not Early, Youre Late

In many parts of Europe, it is customary to arrive for appointments twenty minutes late. Here's a news flash—you're not in Europe!

In North America, you are not only expected to arrive on time for a meeting, you are expected to be there early. When you show up late, you might as well wear a T-shirt that says, "My time is more important than yours!"

Whether consciously or not, customers conclude that salespeople who routinely arrive late for meetings also miss details in the other work they perform.

What the *average salesperson* does:

The average salesperson believes that showing up "around" the time of her appointment is acceptable. She also believes her customers when they say, "It's OK, don't worry about it." What she doesn't realize is that her customer is lying; it really does bother them!

What the *sales superstar* does:

The superstar makes absolutely sure she shows up for every meeting at least ten minutes early. She believes the words of hall of fame speaker Joel Weldon: "If you're not early, you're late!"

And she knows when her customer says, "It's OK," it really isn't.

What can you do?

Make punctuality a priority. Make sure you arrive at least ten minutes early. On those rare occasions when you are going to be late, call ahead and let the other person know. Your message of professionalism will be heard loud and clear!

32. Getting Past the Gatekeeper

One of the most important roles of an administrative assistant is to manage the people who are attempting to speak to his or her boss. As such, they are judged by how they perform, and they get very good at keeping salespeople away.

If you ask a few executive assistants about their opinions of salespeople attempting to speak with their bosses, here is what they have to say.

What the *average salesperson* does:

The average salesperson is too pushy, unprepared, disrespectful, and not honest. I actually cleaned that up a bit. Their opinions were much worse.

What the *sales superstar* does:

The superstar is professional, honest, respectful, and prepared.

What can you do?

Try these techniques to work successfully with "the gatekeeper."

1. *Make a connection.* Use their name and yours. "Hi, Laura, this is Steve" is a lot better than "May I speak with your boss?"

2. *Be honest and respectful.* Their performance with you is important on how they are judged. If they don't trust you, they won't help you.

3. *Use a referral.* If you know someone whom they know, it will help enhance their trust in you.

4. *Ask for their advice.* "Hi, Laura. I know I have called five times now, and I do not want to be a burden for you, so can you help me out? If I do have something I know (your boss) would want to hear about, how do you recommend I go about meeting with him?"

5. *Use humor* (when appropriate).

33. Four to Six Weeks

"How long before I can get the part?" the buyer asked.

"Four to six weeks" the salesperson answered.

Four weeks went by, and the buyer was livid that he hadn't received his order yet. The salesperson pleaded, "I told you six weeks."

"I specifically heard you say four weeks," the buyer said, which ended the argument.

What the *average salesperson* does:

The average salesperson gives ranges when she makes a commitment (i.e., four to six weeks). Then she uses the farthest end of the range (six weeks) as her drop-dead date.

What the *sales superstar* does:

The superstar avoids using a range, but if she does, she uses the shorter time frame to define the commitment (four weeks).

What can you do?

Realize that the buyer only hears what he wants to hear. If you state a range, he is going to lock into the side of the range that benefits him the most. If you don't hit that, you have failed. Your best bet is to not use ranges at all.

34. Not Tonight Perfume

Most perfumes are designed to smell good to attract men. But what is a woman to do when she's not in the mood to attract a man?

Now there is Not Tonight Perfume!

And when "Not Tonight" is *not enough*,

there's Repel!

Seriously? Well, yes, actually!

Companies have been using the strategy of going in the opposite direction for years in order to take major market share.

Apple focused on consumers when all the other computer companies focused on business. Fox News went right when all the other stations had gone left. And Starbucks targeted high-end coffee when the market was competing on price.

What the *average salesperson* does:

The average salesperson follows the market. And trust me, if you're not in the lead, the view is not very good.

What the *sales superstar* does:

The superstar seeks out opportunities to go in the opposite direction and create an entirely new market.

What can you do?

Be bold. Create your own path. You are sure to get much more attention, and it will be nearly impossible for your competition to react.

35. Cynicism

Bob Horn had worked as a salesperson for me for a very long time, and he was a darn good one.

The main reason Bob was so good is because he was so darn optimistic. Nothing got him down. If he got an order, he saw it as the beginning of a trend. If he lost an order, he viewed it as a sign that he would win the next one.

No matter what happened to Bob, he only saw the positive side of it.

What the *average salesperson* does:

The average salesperson is cynical. The cynic believes everyone is out to screw him, every buyer is a liar, and every manager is against him. When he loses an order, he either gets depressed or is ready to quit.

What the *sales superstar* does:

The superstar is an *optimist*. Nothing gets him down. A win is motivation, and a loss is, well, more motivation.

What can you do?

Focus on the positive!

Not only does it keep you going in the right direction, it also attracts customers to you.

For more on the subject read *Learned Optimism* by Martin Seligman.

36. To Be Perfectly Honest

"To be perfectly honest . . . I must be lying!"

A buyer once said that to me right after I said, "To be perfectly honest . . ."

He continued to tell me that every time a salesperson says "I must be honest with you," or "Honestly," or "To be perfectly honest," he thinks the salesperson must have been lying up to that point in the conversation. Why else would the salesperson now clarify that he is telling the truth?

What the *average salesperson* does:

The average salesperson relies heavily on the word *honest* to emphasize a point.

What the *sales superstar* does:

The superstar chooses more effective phrases to emphasize a major selling point or to clarify a surprising response.

What can you do?

When emphasizing a major point, choose phrases like "This is critical," or "I have to emphasize this point," or "I'll circle this one for you."

When clarifying what might be perceived as a surprising response by you, try one of these phrases: "This may surprise you but" or "It may be hard to believe but."

Just don't say "To be perfectly honest" because they may think you are lying too.

37. Im Sorry

"I'm sorry."

I walked into my customer's office and said, "I'm sorry."

He replied with "Dammit!"

"Huh?" I said.

And with a perplexed look on his face, he explained, "I was all ready to lay into you. But I have never had a salesperson come in and just say 'sorry' before. Dammit . . . now I can't throw you out of my office."

What the *average salesperson* does:

When the average salesperson makes a mistake, he gets defensive. He makes excuses, blames someone else, lies, or even worse avoids the customer altogether.

The average salesperson worries that saying "I'm sorry" proves he screwed up.

What the *sales superstar* does:

The superstar doesn't make a lot of mistakes, so when he does, he is not afraid to admit it. When a salesperson makes a mistake, an apology is what the customer wants to hear most. Without it he faces a roadblock; with it he opens the door to further conversation.

What can you do?

Quickly own up to your mistakes, and apologize for them. By doing so, you show confidence, integrity, and even empathy. Those two words, "I'm sorry," can defuse a customer's anger better than any others.

38. Ask for the Order

The two most important lessons I learned as a street vendor are the following:

Lesson 1: Make a connection.

Lesson 2: Ask for the order.

While I stood on the street outside of Rockefeller Center, failing to sell much jewelry, I had plenty of opportunity to observe what the street vending superstars were doing. The good ones always managed to make a connection. The great ones always asked for an order.

It did not matter if they were selling hot dogs, sunglasses, or artwork. The superstars did not end an encounter without saying something like "Would you like one pair or two," or "Can I wrap it up for you right now," or even "Are you ready to buy it now?"

But here is the most important observation I made. When a connection had been made, the customer was actually happy the question was asked! It was almost as if they expected it, and many appeared to feel obligated to reach into their wallet.

What the *average salesperson* does:

The average salesperson is afraid he will offend his customer by asking for an order.

What the *sales superstar* does:

The superstar knows that his customer is actually expecting to be asked and wants you to ask for their business.

What can you do?

Believe it or not, when you develop a relationship with a customer, they want to make *you* happy. Yes, it's true; your customers want to make *you* happy!

They also *expect* you to ask for their business.

39. Bobblehead

The director of marketing handed out bobbleheads to all the salespeople at the meeting. Why bobbleheads, you ask?

Bobbleheads are goofy-looking dolls with heads on little springs so the head bobbles all around.

Strange sales gift for sure, but his point was excellent and hard to forget.

He was urging his salespeople to get past the purchasing agents desk and into the area where all the work was being done.

What the *average salesperson* does:

The average salesperson never gets past the purchasing agent or buyer.

What the *sales superstar* does:

The superstar gets into the manufacturing plant, job site, or wherever his product or service is being used. Once there, he acts like a bobblehead and looks all around for opportunities.

What can you do?

Buy a bobblehead and mount it on your dashboard to remind yourself to get past the purchasing agent. You may be amazed at all the opportunities you find when you walk where the activity is. And situations change, so don't think because you have done this once, you have done it enough.

40. Bad Customers

A lot of salespeople spend waste a lot of time with bad customers.

What the *average salesperson* does:

The average salesperson hangs on to bad customers, hoping that someday they turn into good ones. They fail to evaluate potential and fail to prioritize effectively. Sometimes they are afraid to hand over any customer to a competitor.

What the *sales superstar* does:

The superstar knows where the revenue is and believes that time spent with a great customer will return more than time spent with a bad one. The superstar prefers to have his competitor waste time, so he can concentrate on the biggies.

What can you do?

Measure your ROT (return on time). Estimate how much time you spend on your best customer and what the return is in sales revenue. In other words, if your best customer buys $1,000,000 per year from you and you spend five hours per week with them, your ROT equals $4,000 per hour ($1,000,000 / [5 × 50 weeks]). If your bad customer buys $40,000 per year and you spend an hour per week with them, your ROT equals $800 ($40,000 / [1 × 50]).

Since you have a finite number of hours in a week, the question you must ask is "Will I sell more by spending an hour with a better customer?" If the answer is yes, you need to fire the bad customer. That same hour could generate $4,000 with your best customer versus $800 with your worst.

You should then continue this exercise with all your weaker customers— that's what the superstars do!

Note: This exercise is more effective if you can measure customer profitability and total company time spent with the account.

41. Embellishment

I watched my salesperson embellish and exaggerate point after point to our potential customer. I was not talking, so I was able to observe the body language of the customer and our salesperson. It was not good!

Every embellishment caused the customer to doubt our credibility more. We were not successful, and our salesperson had no idea why.

Committing this sin can tarnish your relationship with a customer forever.

What the *average salesperson* does:

The average salesperson wants the sale so bad he resorts to exaggerating point after point. For many salespeople, this becomes a habit they do without realizing it.

What the *sales superstar* does:

The superstar knows that integrity creates a bond with a customer that can be unbreakable. He also realizes that most customers recognize embellishment a mile away.

What can you do?

Don't do it! Start with self-awareness. Recognize your own embellishment and remove it completely from your approach. Yes, you may lose an order from time to time, but you will win in the long run.

42. Even God Answers My Calls

I read it in a book once. I don't remember which one, but the suggestion was to use humor when you couldn't get someone to call you back. The suggested line was something like this:

Joe, even God answers my calls, won't you?

So I tried it, and it worked. I have since added a few to my repertoire, like these:

Joe, I have been sitting here by the phone for days, sobbing. Won't you put me out of my misery and just call me?

Joe, if you don't call me back, I am going to jump.

What the *average salesperson* does:

The average salesperson calls a couple of times, leaves a message, and then gives up.

What the *sales superstar* does:

The superstar thinks outside of the box and tries something different. She uses humor.

What can you do?

Differentiate yourself with humor. Purchasing people can use some levity every once in a while and tend to respond favorably to those who make them laugh. After you leave your third, unreturned message, try one of the lines above. And if you have any other lines that work, please share them with me at sean@seanleahy.com.

43. Passion

Three men stood around one of those tall bar tables, sipping their drinks and talking about industry mumbo jumbo. This was their third day of a conference, and they hadn't heard anything new in at least two days.

Just then a woman approached them with her own drink. They could tell that she was different. She walked up to the table with a refreshing energy, a smile, and an attitude that said *pure passion.*

The words that followed confirmed that this woman was exactly that . . . *passionate*!

What was she so *passionate* about?

Data!

That's right—data! She ran a data analysis company, and she was *passionate* about it. Her every word captivated the three men because this woman *loved* data and was downright excited about what her company could provide.

What the *average salesperson* does:

The average salesperson becomes bored with the product or service she is selling. Worse than that, she also becomes *boring* when delivering her sales presentation.

What the *sales superstar* does:

The superstar is passionate! She is excited about what she sells, and her delivery becomes captivating to those who are fortunate enough to hear it.

What can you do?

If Denise Keating of DATAgility can be passionate about data, you can be passionate about what you sell. When you are passionate, it is almost impossible for the buyer not to pay attention. Your message also becomes more believable and interesting. Get more passionate today!

44. The Modern Seven-StepB2B Sales Process

If a man walks up to a woman and immediately asks for her number, unless he is Brad Pitt, he is not going to get it.

If that same man is a salesperson and immediately asks his customer for the order, he is going to get the same answer: "No!"

Instead, he must understand there is a process he must follow in order to increase his chances.

What the *average salesperson* does:

The average salesperson is disorganized and just starts selling. He doesn't follow any process.

What the *sales superstar* does:

The sales superstar knows there is a process that, when followed, dramatically increases his odds of success.

What can you do?

Follow these steps.

The Modern Seven-StepB2B Sales Process:

1. **Prepare.** Take the time to plan ahead.
2. **Connect.** Don't start selling right away. Develop a connection first.
3. **Ask.** Ask questions to insure you understand your customer.
4. **Involve.** Get them involved by talking or participating.
5. **Propose.** Provide them with your proposal.
6. **Negotiate.** Any order worth having includes a negotiation. Be prepared for it, and you will be better off.
7. **Close.** Ask for, and get, the business. You deserve it!

45. Rookie Pilot Mistakes

Rookie pilots make more mistakes than veteran pilots do. Sometimes those mistakes are fatal.

Rookie salespeople also make more mistakes than veteran salespeople do. Fortunately for the rookie salesperson, they are rarely fatal, but they can put an early end to an otherwise promising career.

Below is a list of the most common rookie mistakes.

What the *average rookie salesperson* does:

1. Starts late and finishes early
2. Fails to embrace time management
3. Fails to meet all his commitments
4. Fails to strategize
5. Gets down after a loss
6. Forgets his support staff
7. Tries too hard to impress
8. Talks more than listens
9. Fails to cultivate relationships
10. Hides mistakes
11. Fails to ask for the order

What the *sales superstar* does:

The sales superstar acts like a veteran.

What can you do?

1. Start early and finish late.
2. Consistently use a system to manage time.
3. Chew arm off if need be to meet commitment.
4. Set strategy and adjust it regularly.
5. Know that a loss means a win is coming soon.
6. Treat support staff better than you treat your customers.
7. Try harder to be impressed by others.
8. Ask good questions and then shut up.
9. Strive to make valuable connections.
10. Own up to errors and learn from them.
11. Ask for the order . . . every time.

SECTION VIII
RELATIONSHIP SELLING

46. Make a Connection

Ron Whitehead was an ominous 6'4" bald VP of purchasing for Willamette Industries in the mid-nineties. I wanted to take his business away from a competitor, but he repeatedly refused to meet me. Finally, after many attempts, he agreed to a fifteen-minute meeting. I walked into his top-floor corner office overlooking downtown Portland and the Willamette River, and grinned immediately. In a stern voice, Ron said, "What are you smiling about?" I told him that he was the splitting image of my favorite uncle, Uncle Art.

Ron and I then spoke about our families and soon learned that both of our fathers had recently died of cancer. Ron suggested we go down to the restaurant on a lower floor to continue our conversation. Without thinking, I asked Ron if he liked poetry (yes, I know that is a bizarre question to ask). Strangely enough, Ron said yes.

I had written a poem to my father while I sat next to him as he was dying on the hospital bed, and based on what Ron told me about his father, I thought he would find it meaningful. I handed it to Ron to read, and soon after, two 6'4" balding men cried together. After a few more minutes, Ron told me he actually hated his current supplier and said, "Let's go upstairs and work out a deal." It turned out to be an $8-million deal. That's an eight . . . with six zeros . . . due in large part to a poem.

Months later, I realized the significance of this event from a pure sales perspective. *Connection!* I did not realize it then, but I fully understand it now. *Connecting* with your customer on some personal level gives you a significant advantage.

What the *average salesperson* does:

The average salesperson focuses way too much on selling his product or service and often forgets that a human being is sitting across from him.

What the *sales superstar* does:

The superstar knows that every single customer is a person who has a unique set of likes and interests. He also knows that when a customer feels connected with a salesperson, he will often lean heavily in that salesperson's direction. The customer will find you more trustworthy, he will find your offer more appealing, and he will slant his buying decision in your direction.

What can you do?

Be observant, ask questions, and seek out a connection. Whether your kids both play soccer, you both enjoy music, you both stink at golf, or whatever it may be, form a connection with your customer, and you will be ahead of your competition.

47. How to Get a Customer to Like You

People don't always buy from people they like. But people rarely, if ever, buy from someone they don't like. So if you want to sell more, you want your customer to like you, period.

My eighty-year-old friend Joe Howley, one of the most well-liked men I ever knew, shared his advice on the subject with me. He said,

> Don't spend time trying to get someone to like you, let them know you like them. Everyone likes to be liked.

Joe was right!

What the *average salesperson* does:

The average salesperson spends more time talking about business, her product, and her company, and not enough time focused on her customer. If she wants her customer to like her, she often does it by talking about herself and not the person she is with.

What the *sales superstar* does:

The superstar knows that customers buy more from people they like, so she also wants to be liked more by her customers. She does so by using one simple rule:

Let them know you like them.

What can you do?

It's simple. Find ways to let your customers know that you truly like *them*. Listen, be interested in what they say, smile, ask for their advice, call them for nonbusiness reasons, tell them what you like about them, give them a personal gift, applaud their success, find a connection!

48. Ask Their Spouse

We were having an executive strategy meeting at the Admirals Club at O'Hare airport. The room was loaded with C-level executives. Oh yeah, there was a salesman too. We invited one of the best salespeople in the business, Tony Zubizarreta from Houston, Texas.

The question on the floor was "How can we increase sales by 10 percent?" All the executives gave their answers. I don't remember a single one. Then we asked Tony. His answer I can't forget. He said, "I would ask all my customers out for dinner." Everyone laughed.

Then I asked, "What if we had to grow sales by 20 percent?"

Tony's next answer was even more profound. He said, "I would ask them to bring their spouse."

Tony elaborated by saying that all the executives' suggestions were good, but the reason he was so successful was because he developed personal relationships with all his customers. And when his relationship with the customer was strong enough that he knew their spouse, Tony's sales soared!

What the *average salesperson* does:

The average salesperson does not recognize the importance of developing personal relationships with his customers.

What the *sales superstar* does:

The superstar not only develops relationships with his customer, he involves spouses and family whenever possible.

What can you do?

Find ways to involve spouses and family when you entertain your key customers. That will set you apart.

49. The Note

I looked on the credenza behind the customer's desk and saw a line of handwritten thank-you cards. He even had a thank-you letter posted on his wall.

On numerous occasions, people have shared stories with me of great people they have encountered and stated "they even sent me a handwritten note" as evidence.

To this day, I have yet to see a printed out copy of a thank-you *e-mail* on anyone's desk.

What the *average salesperson* does:

The weak salesperson doesn't send any thank-you at all. The average salesperson takes the easy way out and sends an e-mail.

What the *sales superstar* does:

The superstar realizes the impact of being different and going the extra mile. The superstar sends a handwritten thank-you card or letter every time the situation warrants one.

What can you do?

Spend a few bucks and buy some thank-you cards or letterheads. Stock cards are fine, and custom versions are even better. Schedule fifteen minutes on your Friday calendar to send at least one thank-you note for the week. You will be amazed how many times you see your own card on your customer's credenza.

50. Nutritional Value . . . and Humor

After an entire day of showing Steve, the sales trainee, how to sell silicone cartridges, Wayne Donaldson, the sales manager, finally allowed Steve to take the lead.

Steve did a fair job selling right up until his final point. Steve asked the buyer if he was aware of the nutritional value of his product. Since he was selling cartridges, the buyer was very surprised by the question.

"No, I am not," said the buyer, with a confused expression on his face. "What is the nutritional value?"

Steve replied, "If you don't buy this from me, I don't eat!"

After laughing out loud, the buyer gave Steve the order.

What the *average salesperson* does:

The average salesperson often forgets the human side of the business.

What the *sales superstar* does:

Sometimes a little bit of humor can go a long way. A buyer's job can get pretty boring. Breaking up their day with a laugh or two can help in certain situations.

What can you do?

Don't make it your main selling technique, but don't be afraid to use it at the right time either. People like to laugh. It can help break the ice, it can help build relationships, and it can differentiate you from a boring competitor.

51. Logic versus Emotion

Watch a few TV commercials and pay attention to whether or not the advertisers focus on emotion or logic. You will soon find that the overwhelming number of commercials concentrate on your emotional side, not your logical side. That's because they know why most people buy.

While we all realize that many decisions are not made on facts alone, in business we tend to focus 100 percent of our time presenting just the facts.

That's a mistake!

What the *average salesperson* does:

The average salesperson takes the easy path and presents only the facts and benefits.

What the *sales superstar* does:

The superstar takes the time to understand what emotional factors may enter into each and every buying decision. And then he includes an answer to the buyers' emotional needs.

What can you do?

First, study a few commercials or print ads. Then determine what emotional issue the advertiser is targeting. You can use the same mentality in your approach.

What are some of the emotional issues that impact your customers buying decision? Here are a few: relationships, fear of failure, fear of change, indecisiveness, competitiveness, comfort, job security, need for recognition, desire for control, and desire for prestige.

Understand what makes your decision maker tick and be sure to address his needs along with your products' benefits.

52. When in Rome

There is an old saying in business: "When in Rome, do as the Romans do."

Well, our company had a major presentation to give to an extremely important customer, Tyson Foods. Tyson's headquarters is located in Springdale, Arkansas, where they typically wore khakis and polo shirts to work.

We had a debate on whether or not we should wear a suit and tie (because it was an important meeting) or if we should dress more like Tyson dressed.

In the end, we decided to ask the customer what they recommended. Their response: "Whatever you do, *don't wear a suit!*"

We didn't. And we got the order!

What the *average salesperson* does:

The average salesperson wants to impress his customer but makes the mistake of doing so on his own terms. If he thinks a suit is impressive, he wears a suit. He fails to consider what the customer's opinion is.

What the *sales superstar* does:

The superstar is less concerned with impressing someone and is more concerned with making a connection. He realizes that the customer prefers to do business with someone more like himself. If the customer wears a suit and tie, then the superstar may do so as well. If the customer wears jeans, he should consider jeans too.

What can you do?

The safest way to decide is to pick up the phone and ask the customer. That is exactly what we did, and Tyson was happy that we asked.

It was not the reason we were awarded the business, but it certainly allowed them to be more comfortable with us and for us to connect with them.

SECTION IX
PROFESSIONAL SELLING

53. Floodwater

His answer was "Floodwater!"

My question was "What do your best salespeople remind you of?"

He went on to explain that the very best salespeople have one thing in common: they ignore all barriers and relentlessly look for cracks. And once they find one, they break through with raging energy.

What the *average salesperson* does:

The average salesperson focuses on obstacles and gets discouraged all along the way. He acts more like . . . a pond.

What the *sales superstar* does:

The superstar is relentless. Nothing gets him down. He chips away, chips away, until he finds, or creates, a crack. He acts like raging floodwater!

What can you do?

Don't act like a pond; act like raging water.

54. Psychology of Selling?

Bill the salesperson desperately needed this order. It was one of the biggest he would get all year. He would also receive a large commission check for it, and he really needed the money. If he just got this one order, it would make everything in his life easier. He had to get this one . . . no matter what?

At the same time, Jack the buyer was in a horrible situation. His suppliers had recently screwed up a few orders, and projects had been delayed as a result. Key managers within his own company had been complaining to Jack's boss that his tactics either needed to change or he needed to be fired. Jack could not afford to lose his job. He needed this order, which was a biggie, to go right at any cost!

What the *average salesperson* does:

The average salesperson never knows about the issues the buyer is dealing with. He's so desperate, he leads with a low ball offer and writes the business.

What the *sales superstar* does:

The superstar understands the *psychology of selling* and finds out what is going on in the mind of the buyer. Then he delivers what is most important to Jack, not what is most important to himself.

What can you do?

Embrace the importance of "selling psychology." You must put yourself inside the mind of the buyer, probe like a psychologist, understand their issues, and then provide a solution that helps them.

Any psychologist that thinks about himself, rather than his client, soon won't have any clients at all. The same is true for salespeople!

55. Making Copies

Rob the salesman was making copies of his expense report when Carol, another salesperson, called in with great news. She just received another big order!

Rob asked, "How does she keep getting those big orders?"

"Maybe it's because she is out making sales calls," replied one of the customer service reps.

What the *average salesperson* does:

The average salesperson gets bogged down in paperwork and other nonrevenue producing activity!

What the *sales superstar* does:

The superstar makes no excuses and gets his or her butt out the door and sees his customer face-to-face.

What can you do?

Use your cell phone and laptop—from the road! Laptops and cell phones allow salespeople to do more than ever from the road. So if you want to beat your competition, go sell something face-to-face while they're spending time next to the copy machine!

56. Move Over, Accounting

If over half of CEOs in America come through the sales department, why do so many companies allow the accounting department to rule during a tough economy? Sales managers are focused on growth, and accounting managers are often focused on cost containment. So when growth is what is needed most, I say,

Move over, accounting, the sales department is taking over!

What the *average salesperson* does:

The average salesperson will continue to buy into the gloom and doom of the bean counters and other naysayers. The average salesperson will find comfort in having built-in excuses for sluggish sales, and the average salesperson will continue to lose blood, and business, one drop at a time.

What the *sales superstar* does:

The sales superstar will share the attitude of people like Warren Buffett and see opportunities, when others see struggle. The superstar will take advantage of the average salesperson and take business they are willing to lose. The sales superstar will push the accountants aside and announce that this is the year the sales department will reclaim leadership of the business!

What can you do?

You must force the attitude. You must drive positive change, repel negative thinking, ignore the naysayers, and make success happen. You did not go into accounting; you went into sales. Now is the time to act like it!

57. Coyotes, Badgers, and Consultants

A Coyote, a Badger, and a Consultant walk into a room, how do you know which one is the consultant? He is the one with fangs!

Sorry for the consultant humor, supply chain consultants can be tough! But here is a fact about this unlikely group.

When Coyote's and Badgers work together, they improve their results by 30% when hunting Prairie Dogs. That is similar to the story that consultants tell buyers as to why they should hire them to "hunt" suppliers. The truth is that when buyers and consultant's work together, they are also more successful against the supplier.

What the *average salesperson* does:

The average salesperson acts like the Prairie Dog when matched up against a buyer-consultant team. He gets challenged by one and trapped by the other.

What the *sales superstar* does:

The superstar remains poised and composed when faced with the ominous duo. He also knows that the relationship between Consultant and Buyer is often as temporary as is the relationship between Coyote and Badger.

What can you do?

Use your knowledge, plan your approach, and prevent being driven down a rabbit hole and trapped in the dark.

1. Ask the Buyer to clarify the role of the consultant and who the ultimate decision maker is.

2. Ask for the measurement method used to determine the "winner" prior to making your first submission.

3. Your goal for the first submission is to make it to the final round. It is not to provide your best offer!

4. Bring your upper management to "final round" meetings to "even the sides," and to avoid being put on defense.

This simple process can establish you as the Alpha Dog instead of the Prairie Dog.

58. Habit Changer

Have you ever tried to convince a smoker to stop smoking? Or have you ever tried to convince a couch potato to start exercising? Even worse, have you tried to change your own bad habits and failed?

Changing someone's habits is the toughest thing in the world to do. It is even hard when that habit is harmful.

And so it is in sales too. Many of our prospective customers are in the *habit* of buying from someone else. While our competitor may not be their best choice, breaking them of that habit may be extremely difficult.

What the *average salesperson* does:

The average salesperson does not consider the emotional attachment a prospect may have with a supplier.

What the *sales superstar* does:

The superstar realizes that he is also a habit *changer*. And he knows this is a difficult job that requires a different approach.

What can you do?

Follow these five habit-changing steps:

1. Understand your obstacles by asking great questions.
2. Combine patience with persistence.
3. Nibble. You may not be able to win a 100 percent change (patience). You may need to take business away, one nibble at a time. To be successful, you must stay with it (persistence).
4. Work your way up to upper management/the decision maker.
5. Allow the change to be *their* idea.

59. Little Lies

The worst kind of lie ...is a little lie.

During my 26 years in business I have witnessed many, many, salespeople "stretch the truth." My perception is the customer knows a lie has been told 90% of the time. They rarely let on that they know, but they also never forget!

72

The only person who believes a small lie is OK, is the salesperson who told it. The customer believes if a salesperson is willing to lie about something small, he will certainly lie about something "big" too!

What the *average salesperson* does:

The average salesperson believes that a "little lie" is ok to tell as long as it helps get an order. He justifies it as "stretching the truth," or feels that it is not a big deal if it is not a "big lie."

What the *sales superstar* does:

The superstar tells the truth even when it causes him to lose an order. When a customer sees that level of integrity, he knows he can trust the salesperson in any situation.

What can you do?

Tell the truth, or don't say anything at all. Business to business selling is for the long term. Whatever gain you may get by "stretching the truth" in the short term, you will surely lose in the long term.

60. Never Ever Complain to Her Boss

We had gone after this customer's business for years. The lead purchasing agent, "Carol," had a close relationship with our competitor. We just didn't realize how close.

After we delivered what we thought was a slam dunk presentation that included significant savings, we left her office and headed to the airport. Before we returned our rental car, we received a phone call informing us that Carol had given all our information to our competitor.

After much debate, I decided to inform her boss of the unethical behavior of his employee. What I failed to realize is that her boss not only hired her, he trained her, and continued to manage her during this event. Even if he disapproved of her actions, he would never admit it to me . . . never mind doing anything about it. I have never been shut down faster in my life. We were never given a chance at that business again, and I am certain that my comments sealed our fate.

What the *average salesperson* does:

I was the average salesperson that day. I made an emotional decision based on the fact that I was wronged! Looking back, I had made similar mistakes before, going above someone's head when they acted unethically. It never helped. Never!

What the *sales superstar* does:

As hard as it may be, the superstar licks his wounds and moves on. While the superstar may believe that acting as some sort of ethical informant is the right thing to do, it is not his place to do it.

What can you do?

Stop, take a deep breath, wait it out, and never ever, ever complain to her boss!

Inevitably, unethical people do not last long in their positions. Wait until they are replaced and then try again. If they are not replaced, you don't want to do business with them anyway.

61. Read the Room

The deal was worth about $10 million a year. On their side of the table were five trained negotiators and the consultant who trained them. Each of them had a specific area they were responsible for negotiating . . . or should I say, responsible for beating us to a pulp! We had three people on our side, and we really wanted this deal.

After everyone on their side attempted to squeeze every last penny out of us, our lead person asked one question: "Are you serious?"

Then he said, "I am very sorry, but we must respectfully remove our proposal from consideration."

After some discussion, the other side asked for a private meeting. They eventually returned with a request to start the negotiation over.

What the *average salesperson* would have done:

The average salesperson would have caved in.

What the *sales superstar* did:

The superstar read the room. When the consultant spoke, their team's body language indicated a high degree of dissent. They did not agree with the consultant's tactics and their facial expressions spoke volumes. The superstar believed their team wanted the deal as bad as his team did. By withdrawing completely, he hoped the buyers would confront the consultant. It was a calculated risk, and it worked!

What can you do?

Reading the room can be difficult, but it is a critical strength of the very best salespeople. Don't just listen for the spoken word; make sure you are reading body language, facial expressions, and the interaction between people. Many times, the opposition is providing you their most important message . . . in silence.

62. The Cost of Change

In our business, prospective customers often cite the cost of change as a reason to negotiate a better deal out of us. "In order to switch our business to you," they say, "you will need to cover our cost of changing suppliers." It's a pretty good tactic as there actually is a lot of cost associated with switching from one supplier to another.

Just to name a few, switching costs include the following;

1. Setting up the new supplier in their computer system
2. Setting up the accounts payable system
3. Analyzing pricing
4. Identifying and dealing with service gaps
5. Addressing product compatibility
6. Communicating to all that will be affected
7. Handling the product remaining from the previous supplier
8. The cost of the unanticipated. This is often the largest expense.

What the *average salesperson* does:

The average salesperson only deals with the cost of change when they are attempting to sign a new customer.

What the *sales superstar* does:

The superstar uses the cost of change for his own benefit. The star salesperson reminds his current customer of the often forgotten cost of switching suppliers. He uses this information to prevent a customer from moving his business to a competitor.

What can you do?

When you believe a current customer is being approached by a competitor, calculate all the costs they would incur if they were to leave you. Use this information as part of your presentation as to why you should remain as their supplier.

63. Hard Work

I met "Dwight" (not his real name, but the story is true) a few years back at his company's award banquet. Dwight's year was not as good as the year before, but he was still the company's top-performing, top-earning, salesperson. He earned slightly over $1 million that year.

Yes, you read that right, he earned (not sold) over $1 million in one year. He earned $1.7 million the year before!

I asked him what his secret was. Without hesitation he said, "Hard work!"

Dwight said, "I work sixteen-hour days, seven days a week. If one of my customers needs something at 3:00 a.m., they call me."

What the *average salesperson* does:

The average salesperson starts his day a little later and ends it a little earlier.

When given the choice of making the extra call or not, he comes up with a reason to choose "not."

What the *sales superstar* does:

The superstar takes advantage of the average salesperson by out working him. When the other guy is heading home, the superstar is calling on his customer.

What can you do?

The next time you are faced with the question "Should I make that extra sales call?" think of Dwight, and make the call. When you outwork your competition, you will out sell him too!

64. Summary Page

Imagine for a moment that you are the customer, and you just sat through a presentation. It doesn't matter if it was a PowerPoint presentation, a product demonstration, or a presentation across a desk using brochures.

If you are this customer, there is a good chance you are also seeing presentations from other companies. Then you may need to summarize those presentations to other decision makers within your company, and ultimately you will need to review the key points in order to make a decision yourself.

If you were that customer, what you will need most is a summary page.

Yes, a summary page.

What the *average salesperson* does:

The average salesperson gives his presentation and then provides a number of handouts so the customer will have *all* the information on his product or service. Unfortunately the key points get lost within *all* that information.

What the *sales superstar* does:

The superstar makes it easy for his customer. He provides a summary page with only the most important points listed.

What can you do?

Use the power of three rule and identify only your three most important points. Then create a one-page executive summary with only those three benefits listed. Make them big and make them simple.

Include your contact information, and close your meeting by giving it to your customer. You can either use it to ask for the order or use it as a leave behind.

You just made your customers life easier. You made it easier to identify your key strengths, and you made it easier to select you!

65. Put Their Name on It

IDEAL INDUSTRIES made and sold T-strippers forever. T-Strippers are a simple hand tool that strips the coating off of wire so it can be terminated.

One year someone in their marketing department had the idea to put the customer's name on the handle. Then IDEAL sold a ton of T-Strippers. All of a sudden this very simple product became…sexy!

It seemed a lot of companies liked to see their name on stuff.

What the *average salesperson* does:

The average salesperson forgets this age old truth. People not only like to hear their name, they like to see it too!

What the *sales superstar* does:

The Superstar uses her creativity to place her customers name wherever possible.

What can you do?

With today's technology you can easily put names and logos in a wide variety of places. Your PowerPoint presentations should use your customer logo throughtout the presentation. Brochures can easily be personalized with customer names, logos, and images quickly and inexpensively.

If you want to differentiate yourself from the competition, put your customer's name everywhere you can.

66. One Hundred Things the Very Best Salespeople Do

100 things the very best salespeople do...

1. Act as a resource.
2. Act now and apologize later.
3. Adapt to change.
4. Adapt to customer.
5. Admit errors.
6. Admit when customer is right.
7. Always carry a sample.
8. Always write it down.
9. Analyze and solve problems.
10. Anticipate objections.
11. Apologize for mistakes.
12. Appreciate support staffs.
13. Ask the right questions.
14. Ask for more.
15. Ask for the order, often.
16. Be enthusiastic.
17. Be proactive, not reactive.
18. Be prepared.
19. Believe in what they sell.
20. Change direction when needed.
21. Chew arm off if needed.
22. Dispose of bad customers.
23. Do the opposite of competition.
24. Do what they say they're going to do.
25. Earn and use references/testimonials.
26. Eliminate time wasters.
27. Embrace change.
28. Entertain how customer wants.
29. Feed off of rejection.
30. Find the break in the levy and fill it like flood water.
31. Focus on revenue generating activity.
32. Focus on results.
33. Focus on the reward, not risk.
34. Follow up on commitments.
35. Form connections with customers.
36. Get on customer side of table.
37. Get business now, approval later.
38. Get to upper management.
39. Go the extra mile.
40. Hate to lose.
41. Have a system for commitments.
42. Have pride.
43. Improve their own skills.
44. Increase face to face time.
45. Involve customer's family.
46. Judge self on results.
47. Know/present UNIQUE strengths.
48. Know competition better than self.
49. Know product inside and out.
50. Know customer's hot buttons.
51. Let customer know they like them.
52. Listen more than they talk.
53. Look at a loss as inspiration.
54. Make it easy for their customers.
55. Make it fun.
56. Make Buyer look good.
57. Make personal connections.
58. Negotiate from "position of power."
59. Never look back.
60. Over communicate.
61. Paint a picture.
62. Practice.
63. Present Total Value.
64. Prioritize.
65. Provide solutions.
66. Recognize conflict as opportunity.
67. Respond quickly.
68. Say "Thank You!"
69. Seek common ground.
70. 70. Seek growth with current customers.
71. Sell customer profitability.
72. Sell to the decision maker.
73. Sell UNIQUE benefits.
74. Sell with a passion.
75. Send hand written notes.
76. Set goals.
77. Show up 10 minutes early.
78. Smile.
79. Sniff around for opportunities.
80. Start with customer, not selves.
81. Step out of comfort zones.
82. Stop talking when they get order.
83. Structure PowerPoint like sales call.
84. Take chances.
85. Take complete responsibility.
86. Take control.
87. Tell the truth.
88. Think strategically.
89. Think optimistically.
90. Thrive on competition.
91. Treat every opportunity as the last.
92. Understand importance of emotion.
93. Use references effectively.
94. Use ears more than mouth.
95. View objections as opportunities.
96. Walk in faster than they walk out.
97. When in doubt, just do it.
98. Work harder than competition.
99. Work smarter than competition.
100. Worry about the big stuff!
101. Deliver more than promised.

...and 10 things they don't do!

1. Ask customers for favors.
2. Avoid conflict – "sweep problems under the rug."
3. Care about what is fair.
4. Complain.
5. Exaggerate.
6. Give up.
7. Lie.
8. Speak badly about competition.
9. Talk too much.
10. Think they have all of the customer's business.
11. Waste customer's time.

To download a full-size original copy of One Hundred Things the Best Salespeople Do, go to www.seanleahy.com/handouts.

SECTION X
SELLING TO CHARLIE
(SELLING TO UPPER MANAGEMENT)

67. Selling to Upper Management

Have you ever done everything right yet still lost the order? Your price was right, your product was better, and it seemed like the order was a sure thing . . . until you were told at the last minute that your competitor received the business.

Usually that means you weren't selling to the decision maker.

Buyers are generally allowed to make two decisions: "no" and "the decision to continue with business as usual." If you want your customer to change direction, you *need* to sell to upper management.

What the *average salesperson* does:

The average salesperson stays within his comfort zone by selling to the buyer who is assigned to him. When he is told "you better not go above my head," he listens. This is called "buyer block."

What the *sales superstar* does:

The superstar also listens to the buyer but then does what gets him the business. The superstar knows the big decisions are made at the top, and he finds a way to develop those relationships.

What can you do?

When you face "buyer block," it usually means the buyer is afraid to look bad to his boss. The best way to overcome this is by making the buyer look good. Sell the buyer on the benefits he will receive by having you present to upper management. Be sure to include the positive statements you will make about the buyer in front of his superior. Then present to the manager on behalf of yourself and your new partner, the buyer.

68. Five Reasons to Call on Upper Management

First, the five reasons why the average salesperson does *not* call on upper management:

1. **Comfort zone.** The average salesperson spends 90 percent of his face-to-face time with people he knows or people in positions he is familiar with. Average salespeople tend to gravitate to where they are comfortable, and avoid where they are not.

2. **Can't get an appointment.** Either the gatekeeper won't allow access, the manager won't return phone calls, or an appointment is flatly refused.

3. **Buyer block.** The buyer says something like "If you go over my head, I'll kill you!"

4. **Lack of training.** Many salespeople have never been trained on how to get an appointment or what to do once the appointment is made.

5. **Fear.** Without the proper training, calling on top managers can be flat-out intimidating.

Five Reasons Why Sales Superstars *Do* Call on Upper Management

1. **Buyers are allowed to make two decisions.** No, and the decision to continue with business as usual. The superstar knows that in order for a customer to change direction, top management must make the decision.

2. **Who is better at selling your product,** the superstar or an unqualified buyer? If your buyer says *he* will present it to his boss, you are dead!

3. **Eliminate the spinning wheel.** Calling on top management shortens the sales cycle. While average salespeople keep getting delayed by buyers, superstars are pushing a decision with management!

4. **Total Cost** is more important to management. Buyers focus on price, price, price, so the best salespeople go up the ladder to discuss total cost.

5. **You win more!** The salesperson who wins usually has a better relationship with upper management. The one who loses usually doesn't.

69. The Three Things Upper Management Wants to Hear

Knowing that you want to meet with upper management is the easy part. Getting the appointment and knowing what to do once you get there is the hard part.

What the *average salesperson* does:

The average salesperson approaches the manager the same way he approaches the buyer. Without a plan, he calls for an appointment, and if lucky enough to get a meeting, he presents the same way he would to a buyer.

What the *sales superstar* does:

1. He focuses on the three things that upper managers want to hear most about: profit, revenue, and expense reduction.
2. Before he calls for an appointment he prepares a "five-second value statement" that highlights one of those points so he can confidently say it at any time without hesitation.
3. He knows that citing a referral important to the manager improves his odds of success from 14:1 to 4:1.
4. He asks for a fifteen-minute meeting and sticks to it.
5. He focuses on the manager's needs, *not* his own product or service!

What can you do?

Use the upper management planner on the next page or click on www.SeanLeahy.com/handouts to download a form that will guide you through the five-second value statement, getting an appointment, and what to do during the meeting.

Upper Management Sales Planner

Target Manager: | **Company:**
Address 1: | **City**
Address 2: | **State:** | **Zip**
Title:
Phone #: | **e-mail:**
Admin Asst.
Phone #: | **e-mail:**
Referral 1 Name: | **Referral 1 Company:**
Referral 2 Name: | **Referral 2 Company:**

5 Second Value Statement:

☐ Increase ☐ Improve ☐ Reduce/Eliminate ☐ Save

SAMPLE 5 Second Value Statement:

*You can **reduce** your energy costs by 50%!*

Phone Script:

☐ Referral ☐ Their name, not yours! ☐ No "I" ☐ Ask for 15 minutes only

SAMPLE Phone Script:

*"**Your** friend, **John Smith from XYZ**, told me there is a great chance that **you** can save **(your company)** a lot of money. **Your** input is critical! The meeting will absolutely take less than **15 minutes**. What day works best for **you?**"*

First Meeting:
☐ 15 minutes or less ☐ Do NOT Sell ☐ Ask Questions!!
☐ What keeps you up at night? ☐ What would you do if me? ☐ Why do you like us?
☐ Meeting is about THEM, not you! ☐ Make staff look good. ☐ Observe for connections.
☐ Ask for advice. ☐ Take Notes ☐ GET SECOND MEETING!

Second Meeting:
☐ Still about them, NOT YOU!
☐ Profit ☐ Revenue ☐ Expense Reduction

Keeps them up?
If you were me...?
Success?

☐ Ask for the Order!

To download a full-size original copy of The Upper Mgt. Planner, go to www.seanleahy.com/handouts.

70. Straight Shooter

"Straight shooter."

Time and time again, when I ask the question "what makes him or her so good" after being told about a super sales person or business leader, those words were included in the answer.

"Straight shooter."

What the *average salesperson* does:

The average salesperson only tells the story that benefits him. He gives the facts that helps his case and omits those that could, potentially, hurt him. Unfortunately, this style starts to resemble that of the "used car salesman."

What the *sales superstar* does:

The superstar is confident in himself *and* his product or service. He realizes that the customer is attempting to make an informed decision, and he knows that the best customer is the one who is most informed.

Wanting to be the trusted resource, the superstar provides the facts, pro and con and, in turn, gains the trust of his customer.

What can you do?

Shoot straight! Be honest. Tell it like it is. As a manager of salespeople for decades, I have seen it time and time again.

The straight shooters win out in the long run!

ChecklistCalling on Upper Management

UPPER MANAGEMENT CHECKLIST

- ☐ Determine target manager.

- ☐ Research company and manager (Google, Hoovers, etc.).

- ☐ Identify any possible referrals or common acquaintances.

- ☐ Establish your objective.

- ☐ Develop 5 second value statement (increase/reduce).

- ☐ Develop phone script (referral, their name, increase/reduce, 15 minute meeting).

- ☐ First Meeting - Ask questions, learn, make connection.

- ☐ Ask the manager for suggestions on how to work most effectively with his/her organization.

- ☐ Make your main contact look good.

- ☐ Second Meeting - Address issues, solve problems, ask for order.

www.seanleahy.com

To receive a complete pocket-size checklist, go to www.seanleahy.com/sales-checklist.

SECTION XI
NEGOTIATIONS

71. Its All Where You Start

In my training workshops on negotiation skills, I include an exercise where half the audience are salespeople and the other half are buyers. The two sides are challenged to negotiate a deal based on facts that I give to both groups.

What everyone does not know is that I change one, and only one, fact for half of the salespeople. I make their "starting point" higher than the other salespeople. The buyers are completely unaware of the difference.

Inevitably, the salespeople who have the higher starting point also finish with the best deal. It happens every time!

What the *average salesperson* does:

The average salesperson is afraid to insult her customer and scare them off with a high starting price.

What the *sales superstar* does:

The superstar knows and believes in this simple negotiation rule: the number one determining factor on where a negotiation ends is where it starts. She starts higher!

What can you do?

Stretch your comfort zone and start your negotiation with a higher price than you normally do. Starting high not only establishes a higher perceived value, it almost guarantees you better results!

72. Position of Power

The most valuable step in negotiating happens before you enter the room.

The *position of power* is a negotiation concept from Feng Shui, the ancient Chinese practice of studying one's position within one's surroundings. While the original concept had more to do with where you sat, the modern principle relates to being cognizant of your value before you enter the negotiation. This one practice can mean the difference between winning and losing.

What the *average salesperson* does:

The average salesperson enters a negotiation by thinking about what he has to lose. He focuses on the power his customer holds and how little he has.

What the *sales superstar* does:

The superstar focuses on his own strengths. By remaining aware of his position of power, he negotiates with more confidence, gives away less, and comes out ahead more often.

What can you do?

Before entering a negotiation, take out a pen and paper and write down every reason your customer wants to but from *you*. From that list, identify the one or two *unique* advantages that set you apart. This is your position of power. Write it down so you can refer to it when the negotiation gets tough. You will be a better negotiator when you do!

73. If You Could Only Have One Thing

Some customers like to use the "grocery list" technique during a negotiation. Their list may look something like this:

5 percent discount
Early payment discount
Extended payment terms
Rebate

And so on and so on.

One of the most effective counter techniques is to say something like this:

Which one is most important? If you could have only one of these, which one would it be?

What the *average salesperson* does:

The average salesperson either gives into the demands or goes down the list and says no . . . one request at a time.

What the *sales superstar* does:

The superstar finds out what is most important and then focuses his negotiation on that request.

What can you do?

Once the customer tells you what is most important, it then becomes OK for you to assume the other items are not as important. Your next question can be "If I can give you what is most important to you, do we have a deal?" You may be surprised by how well this works!

74. Make Them Look Good

What is the one thing your customer wants out of their negotiation with you?

To *win*!

Everyone wants to win in a negotiation. Your customer is no different. And one of the main reasons that they want to win is so they will look good to their boss.

So one of your jobs is to help your customer look good at the end of the negotiation.

What the *average salesperson* does:

The average salesperson "wins the battle but loses the war." "Winning" a negotiation can actually hurt you if your customer looks bad afterward.

What the *sales superstar* does:

The superstar does not compromise his position in the negotiation, but he does make sure he helps his main contact look good in the end. This helps him close the current deal and makes all future deals that much easier.

What can you do?

Leave your pride at home, but bring your wisdom to the table. When you attain what you want in the negotiation, take special care not to gloat, be overly anxious, or even smile too much. Allow your customer to feel like they have received a great deal and make sure your counterpart looks good in the boss's eyes.

75. The Power of No

One of my first sales training assignments was to sit with a buyer for a few days. It was like hanging out behind enemy lines as I watched other salespeople attempt to sell. At the end of every presentation the buyer asked for a concession. Almost every salesperson gave one.

One, however, said, "No."

The buyer shocked me when he replied, "OK."

When I asked the buyer why he said "OK," his answer shocked me again. He said, "My job is to ask. If I get something, it is a bonus."

What the *average salesperson* does:

The average salesperson feels obligated to give something when a buyer asks for a concession. Some salespeople are either afraid of the consequences or simply don't want to offend the buyer.

What the *sales superstar* does:

The superstar is confident in the value he provides and is confident enough to say, "No."

What can you do?

A confident "No" goes a long way. If the buyer is testing you, a "No" response will expose him. If he is not testing you, more often than not he will ask again. In either case, you have established your position of strength and are in a much better position to negotiate.

76. Pitcher of Water

"Do I need to paint a picture for you?" That is what my mother asked me when I was a boy and did not understand what she was telling me.

That same sentence now comes to my mind when buyers do not understand what I am telling them.

I finally figured out that a picture was exactly what I needed to provide, especially when the subject was difficult for the buyer to understand. And one of the most difficult things to explain to a buyer is why you can't lower their price, extend their payment terms, give them a rebate, and all the other things they are demanding, all at once!

What the *average salesperson* does:

The average salesperson provides the facts in "black and white" terms, hoping the buyer will "get the picture."

What the *sales superstar* does:

The superstar "paints" a word picture that allows the buyer to visualize exactly what you mean.

What can you do?

Ask the buyer to imagine a pitcher of water. The water represents the amount of profit you have available to share. Ask him to also imagine a few glasses. One glass represents a lower price, one represents extended terms, another is for a rebate, etc. Tell the buyer he can pour the water into the glasses, but once the water is gone, you have nothing else to give.

For some reason, this works on most buyers. It helps them visualize that you have a limit on what you can give. This technique has helped close some very difficult negotiations. Used correctly, it could help you too.

77. Why Do You Like Me?

When I was a teenager, I asked a girl I was going out with, "Why do you like me?"

She thought about it and then said, "Actually, I don't like you very much," and she broke up with me.

That question didn't work out for me as a kid, but it has worked much better for me in the business world. During a tough negotiation, for example, the answer to that question can identify *your* position of power.

What the *average salesperson* does:

The average salesperson assumes he knows all his strengths and why a customer is doing business with him.

What the *sales superstar* does:

The superstar knows that situations and opinions change. He also knows the answer to this question gives him insight about his strengths and often provides answers about his competitor's weaknesses (without you asking for it).

What can you do?

You may be surprised at the answers you receive to this question. When you know the *real* reasons why your customer is buying from you, you can use that information to your advantage.

There is also a greater impact when your customer hears himself say why he likes you rather than hearing you say it. And for that reason, you should always ask this question when you are meeting with top management!

78. Put It in a Box

Your customer indicates she wants to buy from you because she asks for the price. So you give it to her. Then she says, "I need you to be 5 percent lower."

If that price is acceptable to you, what should you say?

What the *average salesperson* does:

The average salesperson says, "OK."

And then the customer says, "Great . . . and I also need extra payment terms."

Then the average salesperson says, "OK."

And then the customer says, "Great, and I also need . . ."

What the *sales superstar* does:

The superstar "puts it in a box" by responding with one simple, confining statement. The superstar says, "If I lower my price 5 percent, do we have a deal?"

If the customer says yes, then the deal is made and no other concession is made. If the customer says "No, I also need extra payment terms," the superstar has not committed to anything yet.

What can you do?

"Put it in a box" means getting all the requests identified and "closed" before making any commitment. Make sure you ask "Are these all of your requests?" before making any commitment. Then ask, "Which one is most important to you?" Start with the most important and attempt to close the deal there.

79. The Option

During a negotiation, your customer makes one more demand—let's say for example, they ask for additional payment terms of net sixty days.

If you are not able to give those terms, what do you do?

Do you say no?

What the *average salesperson* does:

That's exactly what the average salesperson says. He says, "Sorry, I can't give you those terms."

What the *sales superstar* does:

The superstar gives the customer an option. She says something like "I can give you net forty-five days if you do X, or I can give you net thirty days if you do Y."

What can you do?

Don't discount this technique because of its simplicity. It works for two reasons: first, because you are not saying no, and second, because it allows them to pick the better of two options. They feel they have "won" the negotiation, even though you got what you wanted.

80. Shut Up

Great leaders are not determined by what they say but by what they *ask*.

Wisdom may not be determined by what one says but by what they *don't say*.

A salespersons success is often determined by knowing when to *shut up*!

What the *average salesperson* does:

The average salesperson is nervous! And the nervous salesperson starts a presentation by talking, talks when other people try to talk, answers his own questions, and is the last person to speak at the end of a meeting.

What the *sales superstar* does:

The superstar is confident, and it takes confidence to be silent.

What can you do?

Follow the rules of when to shut up:

1. After asking for the order
2. After asking any question
3. After saying no
4. After saying yes
5. When someone else is talking or wants to talk
6. When tempted to complain
7. When tempted to criticize
8. When tempted to exaggerate, lie, or mislead
9. When tempted to "top" someone else's story with your "better" story
10. When in doubt about speaking
11. When your customer starts to place the order!

81. The Buyer Might Be Right

Time and time again, I see average salespeople justify a lost sale by blaming it on a bad decision or an incompetent buyer. While it may be true some of the time, it is not the case *most* of the time. More often than not, the buyer makes a decision based on factors that the salesperson simply does not know.

What the *average salesperson* does:

The average salesperson blames others rather than evaluating how his actions may have caused the loss. While this may help him feel better, it does nothing to change the factors that caused him to lose the business.

What the *sales superstar* does:

The superstar doesn't care about feeling better. The superstar is relentless about finding out why he lost, and then he makes the changes to guarantee a win the next time.

What can you do?

Resist the temptation to assume the buyer made a bad decision. Even if the wrong decision was made, find out why it was made. You learn more from your losses than you do from your wins.

82. Ask for More

I love giving up something during a negotiation!

Why?

Because it is the very best time to get additional business!

Almost every negotiation includes some sort of concession. And there is no better time to ask for additional business than right before you are about to give one.

What the *average salesperson* does:

The average salesperson gives in . . . and that's it. When asked for a better price, he gives it and then asks for the order. If he gets the order, he considers the negotiation a success.

What the *sales superstar* does:

The superstar *asks for more*!

It goes something like this:

Customer: "Can you lower your price 5 percent?"

Superstar: "If I lower my price, can I finally get your (additional) business?"

It's that simple!

What can you do?

Ask for more!

Never concede anything without asking for something in return. There is no better time to gain additional business from your customer than when he has just asked you to concede something. You *must* take advantage of the opportunity!

ChecklistNegotiation

NEGOTIATION CHECKLIST

❑ Write down your position of power.

❑ Determine your opening position. (Where you start has the most impact on where you finish).

❑ Determine your desired outcome.

❑ Determine your bottom line.

❑ Give options, not "yes or no."

❑ Determine what you will ask for in return when making a concession.

❑ Ask for more before making any concession.

❑ Isolate what is most important to them by asking "What is the one thing you must have?"

❑ "Put it in a box." Ask "If I say yes to this, do we have a deal," BEFORE making EACH concession.

❑ Shut Up…after each question.

❑ Know when to, and be willing to, walk away.

❑ Make them look good.

www.seanleahy.com

To receive a complete pocket-size checklist, go to www.seanleahy.com/sales-checklist.

SECTION XII
STRATEGIC SELLING

83. Strategy

The definition of *strategy* includes the following words: *science, art, military, enemy,* and *combat.* In short, a strategy is designed to do a serious ass-kicking of the competition and is exactly what is needed in today's business environment! Otherwise, *you* get *your* ass kicked!

Strategy is critical when you have to overcome odds that are stacked against you. In "real" war, it may be a larger army or unfamiliar terrain. In your war, it could be a larger competitor, declining prices, or a shrinking market. Regardless of the challenge, without a strategy, you are destined to follow the market, not beat it.

You are in a war. *You* need a strategy!

What the *average salesperson* does:

Unfortunately, many companies, and most salespeople, forget the strategy part and head blindly down a path to nowhere. They may plan, but they're not sure where they are going.

What the *sales superstar* does:

Once the superstar agrees to an objective, he sits down to develop a strategy *before* he works on a plan. There is a difference—a major difference—and it can determine success or failure.

For example, if your *objective* is to get from Chicago to New York in six hours for under $300, your *strategy* includes the following:

1. *Consider* modes of transportation (i.e., plane, bus, train, car, etc.) and other options.
2. *Analyze* the costs, speed, obstacles, and other factors that will impact your success.
3. *Develop* the best strategy to meet your objective.

What can you do?

Step 1: Make sure you agree with, can succeed at, and are committed to your *objective.*

Step 2: *Consider, analyze,* and *develop strategies* for success.

Step 3: Develop your *plan* on how to get it done!

84. The Opposite Direction

When it comes to developing strategy, many attempt to do something *better* than their competitors. Few have the guts to go in the opposite direction. While doing something *better* may result in gains, going in the opposite direction is where the real growth is!

When CNN decided to enter the news world in 1980, they didn't follow the competition by doing news in thirty- to sixty-minute increments. No, they went twenty-four hours a day and quickly dominated cable news.

Later, when Fox News realized that CNN and the networks all leaned left (liberal), they went right (conservative) and now dominate the market.

When cheap coffee was the buzz, Starbucks went expensive. When high quality and service was the rage, Home Depot introduced lowest price. IBM, HP, and others went after business, Apple went gooey!

They have all done pretty well.

What the *average salesperson* does:

The average salesperson, and company, follows the path worn out by the other sheep.

What the *sales superstar* does:

The superstar has guts! The superstar is willing to lead and forge new paths not yet considered by others. The superstar is the one who winds up with the biggest growth.

What can you do?

Challenge yourself. Analyze where all your competitors are headed. Then brainstorm all the possible ways *you* can do the opposite. Be willing to take the risk and the criticism (all the experts were calling CNN the "Chicken Noodle Network" in the beginning). Then choose the best strategy for your greatest growth. It may be tough, but it could reap huge rewards for you!

85. Attack Customer Strength

Netflix did it to Blockbuster. Scottrade did it to local brokers, and Ronald Reagan did it to Walter Mondale. What did they do? Rather than attack a competitor's weakness, they attacked their strength.

Netflix creatively attacked Blockbuster's dominant distribution channel.

Scottrade attacked the personal relationships brokers had with investors.

And when Ronald Reagan was asked about his age during his second debate with Walter Mondale, he said "I will not make age an issue of this campaign.

I am not going to exploit, for political purposes, my opponent's youth and inexperience." He wound up winning in a landslide.

What the *average salesperson* does:

The average salesperson, and company, follows the old adage of attacking a competitor's weakness. The problem is that if the competitor is weak in an area, it also means there is little to gain.

What the *sales superstar* does:

The superstar wants big gains, and the big gains are where the competitor is strongest. He knows that the competition will not expect to be attacked where they are strongest, and they will also find it difficult to respond.

What can you do?

Identify the large market opportunity that you want to capture. Then identify the competitor who is strongest in that market. Identify each strength they have that allows them to control that market. These are the strengths that you must successfully attack if you have any chance of winning. Your next, and most important, step is determining exactly how you are going to win each battle against each competitor strength.

86. Invite Your Target Customer

Imagine that a car manufacturer asked you to participate in designing their next car. You would have the opportunity to put exactly what you wanted into it. When the car was introduced to the market, do you think you would buy it?

Why not do the same thing with your potential customers?

If you are working on a new program, product, or promotion, why not bring in your largest target customers to help design it. If they design it, it will be very hard to turn you down when you introduce it!

And while you are at it, make sure they are sitting right next to a customer who loves everything about you.

What the *average salesperson* does:

The average salesperson works in a cocoon. He comes up with his ideas and then goes out and sells them.

What the *sales superstar* does:

The superstar uses every possible tool at his disposal. Not only will this technique help you to design a solution that your customers really want, it will instantly give you a customer who is ready to buy it.

What can you do?

You may be thinking, *I am a salesperson. I can't do this on my own.* Yes, you can. Create your own focus group on how you are going to "sell" the new program your company just introduced. Bring in current customers, and target customers, to help "design" your sales approach. Then sell it to them!

87. Mike Tyson

When asked about his opponents plan to beat him, the great philosopher (and professional boxer) Mike Tyson once said, "Everybody has a plan until they get punched in the face." It turns out Tyson is smarter than we thought.

The most forgotten part of a sales plan is the "what if" part. What if the competition actually fights back? Then what?

What the *average salesperson* does:

The average salesperson does not anticipate the next move. When the competition reacts, his plan is over.

What the *sales superstar* does:

The superstar approaches his plan like a chess game and anticipates the reactions of the buyer and his competitors. That way when a reaction happens, he is ready with his next move.

What can you do?

Include the words *what if* in your business plan. Write down every possible response to your original plan and then develop your move for every response. Your chances of success will skyrocket!

88. Recalculating Route

My GPS spoke to me shortly after I started driving. It said, "Recalculating route." Then it adjusted its original plan, so I would, once again, be on course to my final destination.

Soon after you start your year, you probably need some recalculating too.

What the *average salesperson* does:

The average salesperson creates an annual plan to appease his boss and doesn't look at it again until year end.

What the *sales superstar* does:

The superstar is absolutely committed to getting to his target. He then acts as his own GPS, constantly monitors his progress, and makes adjustments to ensure that he stays on course.

What can you do?

Pull out your annual plan. Ask yourself if you are on course to hit all your goals. If not, ask yourself, "How am I going to get there *now*?" and "What do I have to do differently?" Then make the changes and start moving on your new plan. And while you are at it, put a reminder into your calendar to do the same thing every month. If you don't, you will continue to be off course the entire year.

SECTION XIII
FOR THE SALES MANAGER

89. Phil Jackson

Have you ever seen Phil Jackson, former coach of the Los Angeles Lakers, coach from the bench? Sometimes I'm not sure he knew there was a game going on.

So how did he win so many championships?

Michael Jordan and Kobe Bryant, that's how!

I hate to break it to all of you sales managers out there, but the same is true about your team. The very best sales managers have one thing in common—they have the very best salespeople on their team, period.

What the average *sales manager* does:

The average sales manager settles for his current roster of salespeople.

What the star *sales manager* does:

The star sales manager's top priority is having the very best salespeople on his team. He knows there is nothing else that will guarantee his success more than that.

What can you do?

Start by making a commitment to hire the very best salespeople for your team. Then make sure you are motivating your star salespeople so as to keep them on your team. Move the nonperformers off of your bench.

90. Veteran Managers

Rookie pilots have a tendency to become "glued" to their instruments and often forget to look out the window to see what is really going on. For some reason, veteran managers develop the tendencies of the rookie pilot.

Managers often rely on reports and numbers for all the answers. They forget to "look out the window," or even worse, "step out the door," in order to see what is actually happening with their business.

What the average *sales manager* does:

The average sales manager sits behind a desk and reviews data, reports, and call reports. He rarely goes out and visits customers.

What the star *sales manager* does:

The star manager is out of the office more than he is inside of it. The numbers only tell part of the story. No report will ever replace the intelligence attained while sitting with a customer.

What can you do?

Get up from behind your desk and get out of the office. You will be smarter, be more in touch, and have much greater impact on your sales team and your business.

91. Three Types of Salespeople

If you Google "types of salespeople," you will find many descriptions: closers, order takers, problem solvers, hunters, farmers, etc.

Here's my list: *superstars*, *role players*, and the *cut list*.

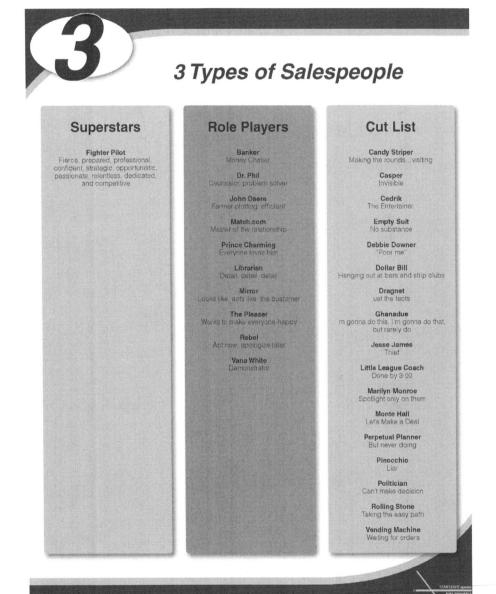

3 Types of Salespeople

Superstars

Fighter Pilot
Fierce, prepared, professional, confident, strategic, opportunistic, passionate, relentless, dedicated, and competitive

Role Players

Banker
Money Chaser

Dr. Phil
Counselor, problem solver

John Deere
Farmer-plotting, efficient

Match.com
Master of the relationship

Prince Charming
Everyone loves him

Librarian
Detail, detail, detail

Mirror
Looks like, acts like the customer

The Pleaser
Works to make everyone happy

Rebel
Act now, apologize later

Vana White
Demonstrator

Cut List

Candy Striper
Making the rounds...visiting

Casper
Invisible

Cedrik
The Entertainer.

Empty Suit
No substance

Debbie Downer
"Poor me"

Dollar Bill
Hanging out at bars and strip clubs

Dragnet
ust the facts

Ghanadue
m gonna do this, I'm gonna do that, but rarely do

Jesse James
Thief

Little League Coach
Done by 3:00

Marilyn Monroe
Spotlight only on them

Monte Hall
Let's Make a Deal

Perpetual Planner
But never doing

Pinocchio
Liar

Politician
Can't make decision

Rolling Stone
Taking the easy path

Vending Machine
Waiting for orders

To download a full-size original copy of Three Types of Salespeople, go to www.seanleahy.com/handouts.

You may argue that those listed as role players can be superstars, and you may be right. But the best of the best are the fighter pilots. If you want to have the very best team, you must have them on your side. You cannot, and will not, be the best without them!

Just as important, you must cut those on the cut list. Some studies show that great salespeople can be 67 percent more effective than their weaker counterparts. Keeping them not only hurts your sales, it demoralizes your superstars.

What the average *sales manager* does:

The average sales manager accepts his team and does not constantly seek to improve its players.

What the star *sales manager* does:

The star manager fills his roster with as many stars as possible. He knows what qualities he needs and where he needs them, and he makes sure he fills the right roles with the right people.

What can you do?

Start by assessing your sales team. Identify the stars, role players, and who needs to be cut. Then identify where your holes are and where you need to upgrade and where you need to cut. Then do it!

92. Finding the Sales Superstar

You have decided you want to add superstars to your sales team, so how do you go about doing it? Here are the keys:

1. Think like a general manager of a sports team. They do this better than any business.
2. Have a great team to start with. Stars want to be on the best team—it makes recruiting a lot easier.

3. Use your best players to recruit other great players. For some reason, they know each other.
4. Ask your best customers for referrals and recommendations. They also know the top salespeople.
5. Develop a strong interview and hiring process.
6. Treat your stars like stars.

What the average *sales manager* does:

The average sales manager places ads, accepts resumes, interviews a few candidates, and hires the person he likes best.

What the star *sales manager* does:

The star manager is committed to hiring the best, only the best, and places this activity as his number one priority. He takes his time to aggressively recruit, and he does not settle for mediocrity.

What can you do?

First make the commitment. Next, develop an employee referral program. Then reach out to the stars on your team, your best customers, and everyone else who you feel can provide great recommendations. Follow that up by improving your interview and hiring process. Then work your butt off to hire her! Everything else you do becomes a lot easier once she is on your team.

93. Interview Question for Sales Superstars

Here are ten questions to help determine if your candidate is a superstar, a role player, or on the cut list.

1. What are the three main reasons people buy from you?
2. Did you choose sales or did sales choose you? Why?
3. What do you love most about sales?
4. Tell me about your sales/follow-up system.
5. Would you rather go after new accounts or call on existing accounts?
6. What are your thoughts on calling on upper management?

7. What is the one question you hoped I would not ask you?
8. Tell me about the most grueling sales experience you have ever had.
9. Tell me about your worst loss? Why did you lose? What did you do?
10. Please finish this sentence: "My sales style can be best described as…"
11. How did you prepare for this interview?

To download a full-size original copy of Thirty-Five Interview Questions for the Sales Star, go to www.seanleahy.com/handouts.

What the average *sales manager* does:

The average sales manager wings it. He jots down a few questions and then asks the candidate. Then he uses his gut instincts to decide if he likes the guy or not.

What the star *sales manager* does:

The star manager knows exactly what characteristics and traits he is looking for. He then asks specific questions that will identify if the candidate meets his requirements. Then, if the candidates meet his requirements, he hires them. If not, he keeps on recruiting.

What can you do?

First, go to www.seanleahy.com/handouts for a complete list of thirty-five great questions to use in a salesperson interview. Divide the questions up among three people who will make up your interview team. Use the responses to determine how well the candidate matches each of the qualities you are seeking (i.e., prepared, relentless, etc.). When you have the person who meets your requirements, hire them! For extra help, I highly recommend Culture Index (www.cindexinc.com). Their profile testing provides exceptional clarity for hiring exceptional salespeople.

94. The Sandwich

I don't care if you are talking to a truck driver or if you are talking to a CEO, this approach works.

If you have times when you have to criticize, complain, or disapprove of the work someone else has done, ultimately you are attempting to bring them around to your way of thinking.

The very best approach is "the sandwich."

What the average *sales manager* does:

The average sales manager loses her head and goes straight to the criticism. It sounds something like this: "Jim, I just heard that you screwed up another order, can't you do anything right?"

What the superstar *sales manager* does:

The superstar manager understands that criticism alone does nothing to improve the situation. He knows the ultimate goal is to improve the behavior and the results of the person he is speaking with. The superstar uses "the sandwich" technique.

What can you do?

A real sandwich is made with a slice of bread, the meat, and another slice of bread. The criticism "sandwich" is made up of a positive statement, the criticism, and another positive statement. It sounds something like this;

"Jim, I know you have been working your butt off this week, and I really appreciate that.

But Jim, I just received another complaint about an error you made.

I know I can count on you to improve this situation."

It is simple, but highly effective . . . at all levels.

95. The Crusade

Once you have superstars on your sales team, you then want to keep them. There are a number of ways to do that, but one stands above all the rest: *success.*

Think of star athletes—they all want to win a championship. They all want to be on successful teams. They all want to win, win, win! Your job as their manager is to create an environment that challenges them and allows them to win. I like to call it the *crusade.*

What the average *sales manager* does:

The average sales manager sets the goals at the beginning of the year and reports the progress throughout the year.

What the star *sales manager* does:

The star manager creates a *crusade!* Winning becomes a must! The journey is an *event! Success* comes with meaningful rewards and celebrations!

What can you do?

Start your crusade right now! It does not matter where you are in your fiscal year. Start your crusade for the balance of the year. Get creative. Make it a challenge. Make it fun. Most importantly, make it competitive. Constantly post the results and who is winning and who is not. Your fighter pilots will "compete to the death" in order to win.

96. Act Now, Apologize Later

After Jack received The Salesperson of the Year Award, the President of the company asked Jack a few questions on stage.

President: Jack, what is the main reason for your success?
Jack: My act now, apologize later, approach.

President: (surprised) But can't that backfire and get you in trouble?
Jack: Yes.

President: Then why do you do it?
Jack: Because it can also win me this award!

What the *average salesperson* does:

The average salesperson is overly concerned with rules and what the right thing to do is. While I may respect them for their high level of integrity, I also prefer that they work in the accounting department.

What the *sales superstar* does:

The superstar acts now and apologizes later. Part of me hates to admit it, but the reality is that it is true.

What can you do?

As a sales manager I hate when my salespeople ask for forgiveness rather than permission.

But as a sales manager I love when I have salespeople who ask for forgiveness rather than permission.

Huh?

That's right, I hate when they do it, but I also know that is the personality type that makes the best salespeople. They make things happen!

I am not suggesting being unethical. I am urging pragmatic decisions being made quickly. Great salespeople are aggressive and smart. Be both and you will win many battles while the other guy is pulling out the rule book.

97. Priceline

(Note: The following Sales Shot received many emotional responses after I first published it. I assure you that this is not a commercial and I have not received any type of compensation for it. I do not know anyone at Priceline…I simply love their service.)

Today, I am the president of a company. As such I travel a lot. While on the road I like to be comfortable, but I like saving money even more. So when I make hotel reservations, I use Priceline.

The amount of money I save with Priceline is mind boggling.

If you want to save money, reduce costs, and help free up space on your budget, I suggest you give Priceline a shot.

What the *average salesperson* does:

The average salesperson either pays too much for hotels or stays in low-end hotels to keep his costs down.

What the *sales superstar* does:

The superstar uses Priceline when making hotel reservations.

What can you do?

Go to www.priceline.com or download the app to your smartphone. Go to the "Name Your Own Price" section on their home page and give it a shot. I often save 40 to 50 percent on hotel rooms.

SECTION XIV
MORE REASONS WHY SALESPEOPLE ARE LIKE PILOTS

98. Pilot in Command

A few years back I took my first flying lesson . . . and I was *nervous*!

As I stopped short of the runway, right before I was about to takeoff for the first time, my flight instructor asked me what I did for a living. Strange question indeed.

I said, "Sales . . . Why?"

He answered with "Sean, flying an airplane is a lot like sales."

"Oh really," I asked. "How's that?"

He said they were similar in three ways. "The first way," he said, "is you, and you alone, are pilot in command. Just like in sales, you have all kinds of people helping you. You have inside sales, accounting, marketing, and even your boss. As a pilot you will have ground control, air traffic control, flight watch, and you have me sitting right here next to you. But most importantly remember this—despite all the help you have, you, and you alone, are pilot in command. You are ultimately responsible for *you*."

What the *average salesperson* does:

The average salesperson is quick to blame others within his company for his lack of sales. The price is too high, the product is not good enough, customer service fails to meet expectations, and on and on and on.

What the *sales superstar* does:

The superstar takes responsibility. He knows that the only person he can control is himself.

What can you do?

Utilize all the support that you can get by others within your company, but view it as just that—support. Take ownership of your own success, and you will have much more of it.

99. Have a Plan

My flight instructor then told me the second way that flying was a lot like selling. He said, "Just like in sales, you must have a plan, you must write it down, and you must keep it with you at all times. But most importantly you must remember this—your flight, like every flight, will be off course 95 percent of the time.

In order to stay on course you must constantly monitor your progress and make adjustments all along your route. If you do, you will land safely at your final destination. If you don't, you'll never get there."

What the *average salesperson* does:

The average salesperson creates a plan and then files it away and never looks at it again.

What the *sales superstar* does:

The superstar acts like a pilot and constantly adjusts his plan based on events that knock him off course.

What can you do?

Once you finalize your annual plan, enter reminders into your calendar to check your progress. At a minimum, reevaluate your plan at the end of each month. Then make adjustments so that eventually, just like a pilot, you eventually land safely at your final destination.

100. There Is No Reverse in This Airplane

My flight instructor then told me the third reason that flying was a lot like selling. He said, "There is no reverse in this airplane!

"Once you make the decision to go, there is no turning back!"

What the *average salesperson* does:

The average salesperson never makes a full commitment. Not only does he fail to push the throttle all the way forward, he continually looks back and considers abandoning his mission.

What the *sales superstar* does:

The superstar goes *full throttle*!

What can you do?

Once you make a commitment, don't look back. Looking back not only prevents you from seeing the obstacles in front of you, it also stops you from seeing your final target.

SECTION XV

101

101. Promise a Lot and Deliver More

This is sales shot # 101. The cover of the book states that there are 100. That is because the best salespeople deliver more than they promise.

What the *average salesperson* does:

The average salesperson promises a lot and delivers less. He tends to embellish, exaggerate, and sometimes even lie.

What the *sales superstar* does:

The superstar follows this simple rule with a vengeance:

Promise a lot and deliver more!

What can you do?

Follow this rule with every bit of energy you have. When you do, your reputation will precede you, your customers will become loyal to you, and you will be a sales superstar!

Thank you for reading *The Sales Shot*! If you liked it, please pass it on to others. If you didn't, please pass it on to others anyway.

If you would like to receive a free sales shot every week or two via e-mail, please sign up at **www.SeanLeahy.com/signup**.

To learn more about hiring me to speak at an upcoming meeting, please visit **www.SeanLeahy.com**.

Thank you!

—*Sean*

ABOUT THE AUTHOR

After finishing high school in the bottom half of his class, Sean tried his hand at selling cheap jewelry on the streets of New York City... and he failed miserably. But as a result, he had plenty of time to stand back and watch the vendors who were cashing in. He started taking notes on what the successful salespeople were doing, and what he wasn't. In order to pay his way through college he sold gas grills, cassette tapes, stereo equipment and worked the midnight shift at a convenience store. Encountering both success and failure, Sean learned from every experience, and his hunger for success grew stronger.

In 1996 Sean started The VAN TAGE GROUP, a company made up of some of the largest suppliers in the electrical industry.

Today, Sean is the President and CEO of Vanguard National Alliance, a consortium of Rockwell Automation distributors throughout North America.

In the past 3 decades Sean continued keeping notes on what the best sales people were doing and what others weren't. Although he now has thousands of notes, Leahy has taken his 100 best tips and compiled them into this book.

Join the close to 100,000 sales professionals from around the world who read The Sales Shot every week.

Made in the USA
San Bernardino, CA
06 November 2013